BLACK ASH, ORANGE FIRE

for Jim & Cynthia —

who were helpful
during the initial ms.
stages and who have
been longtime and
good friends

Bill Witherup
July 26, 1986

Also by William Witherup:

This Endless Malice, Twenty-five poems by
Enrique Lihn. Co-translated with Serge Echeverria.
(Lillabulero, 1970)

I Go Dreaming Roads, Selections from
Antonio Machado. Co-translated with Carmen Scholis.
(Peters Gate Press, 1973)

Arctic Poems by Vicente Huidobro. Co-translated
with Serge Echeverria. (Desert Review Press, 1973)

Black Ash, Orange Fire
Collected Poems 1959–1985

by
William Witherup

With a Foreword by
William Everson

and

an Afterword by
James B. Hall

FLOATING ISLAND PUBLICATIONS
POINT REYES STATION
1986

Published by:

Floating Island Publications
P.O. Box 516
Point Reyes Station, California 94956
ISBN: 0-912449-15-2

Cover illustration by Cornelia Schulz

Acknowledgements:

The poems in *Black Ash, Orange Fire* have been culled, for the most part, from the following chapbooks: *Horsetails*, with Stephan Taugher (Peters Gate Press, Monterey, 1970); *Love Poems* (Peters Gate Press, 1971); *Private & Public Poems* (Peters Gate Gress, 1972); *The Sangre de Cristo Mountain Poems* (Lillabulero, Northwoods Narrows, New Hampshire, 1970); and *Bixby Creek & Four from Kentucky* (Uzzano Press, Mt. Carroll, Illinois, 1977).

Anchor/Doubleday in *Quickly Aging Here, Some Poets of the 1970s* (Doubleday & Company, Garden City, New York, 1969) included these poems: "On the Death of Theodore Roethke"; from "Three for Robert Bly"; "A Gothic Tale"; "The Great White Father"; "Marian at Tassajara Springs"; and "Freeway."

"Freeway" also appeared in the anthology, *Live Poetry* (Holt, Rinehart and Winston, New York, 1971). "Depression" was published in the anthology *The Now Voices* (Charles Scribners Sons, New York, 1971).

Thanks and credits are also due to the following literary magazines and quarterlies where some of the poems in *Black Ash, Orange Fire* first appeared:

Abraxas, American Poetry Review, Appalachian Heritage, The Back Door, California Oranges, Changes, Dacotah Territory, Dragonfly, Fragments, The Freelance, Greenfield Review, Desert Review, Hearse, kayak, Lillabulero, Madrona, Mountain Review, New American & Canadian Poetry, New Mexico Quarterly, North Coast Poetry, Northwest Review, Poetry Northwest, Poetry Now, Poetry Pilot, Portland Review Magazine, Prairie Schooner, The Nation, Rumours, Dreams and Digressions, Searchcraft, Sur, Scree, Stinktree, Tolar Creek Syndicate, Transfer, Trace, Uzzano, Vigencia, West Coast Poetry Review, White Pine Journal, and *Fairfax-San Anselmo Children's Center Newsletter*.

Publication of this book is made possible, in part, through a grant from the National Endowment for the Arts in Washington, D.C., a federal agency.

To my mother, who bore me
and my father, who bore with me.

Contents

In San Francisco

from The Sangre De Cristo Mountain Poems

Kentucky

Images From A Marine Landscape

Monterey

Soledad

Cities of Assassination

from I Go Dreaming Roads

A Foreword by William Everson

Landscape determines. Were a mere axiom capable of pin pointing the flux and contour of West Coast sensibility it would have to be some such attestation to the power of the place. The gigantic scale of its distances, the relative thinness of its population, the elevation of its volcanic peaks, the ploughshare ridges of its vast glacial sierras, the immensity of ocean hammering its shores—from the Puget Sound rain forests to the stark aridity of Baja, California, the Pacific Slope is characterized by a landscape that overwhelms human life and shapes its responses. Its poets might almost be thought of as gifts nature renders back to man in compensation for its monumental disdain. They serve as the gutteral of an unheard music transcending speech.

William Witherup, born in Kansas City in 1935, grew up in eastern Washington where the distances are enormous and the climate severe. In high school he aspired to the Methodist ministry, but desultory attempts at college did not confirm this calling. Rather it was as a sophomore at the University of Washington that he chanced into Theodore Roethke's verse writing class. Not having read the poet, it was the presence of the man himself—intense, committed, somehow personifying a higher consciousness—that spoke to the youth. In Roethke the office of poet emerged as an exercise in psychic realization exceeding anything he had encountered in life and, recognizing the need in himself, his vocation was indicated.

However his restlessness of quest was not over. Drifting south he studied under James B. Hall at the University of Oregon, acquiring the strategies of direct literary engagement, and then migrated to California where he arrived in the wake of the acclaimed San Francisco Renaissance. Here he imbibed that admixture of Zen, Amerindian and backcountry perspectives which currently form the Californian contribution to Pacific Basin culture. It was his moment of confirmation. The awesome, charismatic witness of Roethke, the meticulous technique of Hall and finally his adoption among kindred spirits into the San Francisco ambiance ineluctably coalesced, confirming him a poet in his own right. From this point on his contribution becomes distinctive. Now, with *Landscapes*[1], he joins the groundswell of West Coast writing.

These shaping elements are perceptible in his verse. An unwavering commitment to the craft of poetry and a scrupulous respect for technique stand behind his humbleness before the ingredients of Western communal life. In this, of course, he is not original. From one point of view he simply employs the well-known practices made accessible by Gary Snyder. This emphasis differs from the older generations of West Coast poets like Jeffers, Rexroth and myself, lately joined by Bill Hotchkiss, whose *Fever in the Earth* picks up Californian verse narrative where Jeffers left it. All our work derives from the historic romantic tradition through Whitman and D. H. Lawrence, the approach to nature being essentially descriptive and panoramic. In the poets following Snyder, on the contrary, there is an adaptation of modernist perfectionism stemming from Pound to the Zen perspectives of implication and indirection, a poetry engagingly open in form but tersely closed in internal compression. If this makes for minor verse ill-adapted to sustained expression it compensates through penetrating insight and haunting evocation. Although Witherup disclaims any conscious stylistic derivation from Snyder, it is evident that his accommodation to the dominant method which changed the focus of West Coast writing defines his sector.

What, then, does he bring to this practice that is uniquely his own? Nothing technical, I think: he is not an innovator. Rather, the answer lies in a certain truth to inner response that lets both technique and materials dissolve before subjective reality. His technique rarely obtrudes on his meditation. Or rather his technique at its best has been subsumed into his meditation until it unconsciously defines it. He has learned how to enter a poem, inhabit it, and then happily forego it. Within this clearly maintained stylistic limitation he goes about the poet's true business of transmuting indigenous materials into perceptive revelation.

This is as much the work of his ear as of his eye. He himself speaks of his verse as essentially imagistic. I, however, hear his music, which is the vibration of his sensibility, his feeling. He searches for meaning in the response which his encounter with nature (and with women) arouses in him. Shy, circumspect, his involvement is appealingly tangential. But his instinct prevents him from self-consciously smoothing the roughness out of his materials, being natively humanist in the grassroots Western way. Skeptical of civilization, disgusted with its discontents, in him the reformist vein in West Coast writing finds outlet through an occasional tirade against polluters of every stripe, but this is not his strength. His strength is the impulse that moves his shyness to find its voice in understatement, the art that leaves implication suspended until its images explode in depth.

To sum up, in Witherup we find the pervasive Western landscape interiorized rather than projected. We get landscape *felt*, experienced not through how it appears but in what it does to a man, its meaning resonating inwardly on the secret lyre of sensibility. We get humanity in the form of a poet marrying landscape like a shy awkward lover, a lover unsure of his love as of himself, but preternaturally certain that his feeling will find its term and be realized. It is this unspoken assumption which constitutes the authority with which he writes.

November 25, 1978
Kingfisher Flats
Swanton, California

[1]The manuscript was originally titled *Landscapes*. The foreword is included in William Everson's *On Writing the Waterbirds and other Presentations. Collected Forewords and Afterwords, 1935–1981*. Scarecrow Press, Metuchen, N.J., 1983.

Preface

It may be arrogant to collect one's own poems while still alive and call it "The Collected Poems." Nevertheless, I have done it — mostly to give myself a stopping and starting point for future endeavors.

I have included as the last section in the book a selection of translations from the Spanish poet, Antonio Machado, which appeared previously in a limited edition chapbook of two hundred copies. Of the three Hispanic poets I have had a hand in translating, Machado was the closest to my own spirit at the time of translation. Along with reading Kenneth Rexroth's *One Hundred Poems from the Chinese*, having to give Machado a close read was the second formative influence on the Big Sur poems, which a few people consider my best work.

I could not have translated Machado without the help of Carmen Scholis, who was also my companion for five years in Monterey and Big Sur. Which also brings to mind something Machado said in an essay: the poet does not write the poem alone. Women, children, friends, the entire culture have a hand in it.

I have named directly in some of the poems, and in dedications to some of the poems, wives, lovers, friends and our many and various children. The list might go on for a full page. I would like then to name a few people who were instrumental in catalyzing the book at hand and who are not named in the poems.

Poets Michael Hannon and Mike Tuggle read the manuscript and gave helpful suggestions. Tuggle recommended the manuscript to my publisher, Michael Sykes, during a period when I was in a state of despair and depression. William Webb of Big Sur was the initial catalyst for the earlier version, *Landscapes*. After he encouraged me to get it together, he hand carried it to Farrar, Strauss and Giroux, where it was turned down because I was too much a *western* poet. It was Webb who also suggested his friend, William Everson, write the "Foreword." James B. Hall, my mentor at the University of Oregon in 1956–57, asked to come aboard and write an "Afterword" for the revised edition. He was also a hard editor in helping me edit out some of the weaker poems. I would also like to thank Judith Ayn Bernhard for looking over and currying the final manuscript.

Had I not dedicated the book to my parents, I would have dedicated it to my high school art teacher and yearbook advisor, James McGrath. It was McGrath and mad Hanford that hurt me into poetry.

Otherwise, the "Prologue" from the Restoration play by Sir John Vanbrugh expresses what it is like having chosen the profession of Poet. Please tell me, with the small profits of publishing poetry, where to eat.

—William Witherup
San Anselmo, California
January, 1986

Prologue

Spoken by a shabby poet

Ye Gods! what crime had my poor father done,
That you should make a poet of his son?
Or is't for some great services of his,
Y'are pleas'd to compliment his boy—with this?
[Shewing his crown of laurel]
  The honour, I must needs confess, is great,
If, with his crown, you'd tell him where to eat.

Sir John Vanbrugh
"The Confederacy"

Dreams & Fetishes

At Malya, Crete: 1959

"We are a dream in the mind of God."
— Spinoza

In a dream agony your image rises
from the bottom of my psyche,
rises like a sprig of pink coral fern
torn from a grotto in a sea swell,
rises to float upon my mind's surface
and troubles me from sleep.

Waking I hear the windmills turning
and, above the hissing swells,
bathers' laughter.
Often I dream a darker dream:
sunning or loving by the sea
our pleasure was another dreamer's pleasure.

A Fable

When antelope first saw Men—
hairless, on their hind legs,
moving in a line across the veld—
a new terror ran in the animals' veins.

The lions, watching from the bush,
did not like the smell and slipped away.

But the hyenas were pleased
at the arrival of the Upright Ones,
and rolled ecstatically
in vomit and rotting meat.

An Australian Dream

The darkness
is luminous
in Australia
The sand
seethes with
yellow moonlight
Jackals and hyenas
tear through
the outback
kicking loose
bird skulls
and skeletons
of rabbits
My father
My father
once a jolly swagman
has come
to this
has come
to this
is dressed
in black
like a
Spanish priest
wears a
black robe
and a
wide brimmed
hat; poles
a leaking
punt through
black water

An American Dream

The Paiute in Modesto
talked of his new orange tractor
and of his peaches ripening in the sun.
We walked out to see his orchards,
shielding our eyes against the light,
to find the branches crusted with maggots
and the fruit dripping.
"America, America, America," he wept.
As I put my arm around his shoulders
the darkness rushed in,
leaving us in an empty field bordering a freeway.
It trembled and we knew we had to cross it.
We stepped over the shoulder,
our faces clay masks beneath the blue arc lights,
and the freeway closed behind us
with the faint whirring of a theater curtain.
As we walked into the darkness
the gourd rattles of the Eternal Ones
began to sound the night like crickets.

Messages from a Zuñi Fetish

1

An alabaster bear
with a turquoise arrowhead
strapped to its back with sinew
stands on my writing desk.

On fortunate days
the desk becomes an altar
covered with plume wands
and *tablitas* of clouds, lightning and corn.

When I open my ledger to write
it crumbles like an old parflêche bag.

2

Each night Zuñis creep through my room
with drawn bows
to kill the albino grizzly
who has his will of their corn fields,
rifling the largest, sweetest ears.

The warriors' odor
mingles with the milky scent of corn;
the moonlight on the corn tassels
and on the plumed tassels of the bows
is like music.

I would like to reach out
and touch the nearest man on the arm,
but a stronger love goes out to the bear
and I snap a stalk to frighten him away.

The Zuñis turn and look at me
as if they'd known my presence all the time.
I search for words to explain what I have done
and why I am there,
but the men slip away
into the deep shadows of the corn rows.

3

I come disguised as the Plumed Serpent,
my raft moving over water as black as obsidian.
With the wind and moonlight in my feather cape
I feel as strong as a white breasted sea eagle.

Moctezuma waits on the steps of his palace,
arms outstretched to receive me, like a lover.
His wrists are adorned with gold bracelets;
his hair scented and oiled.

He trembles slightly and looks uncertain
as he notices my blue eyes
and the paleness of my skin,
which is the color of holy wafers.

In my sash is a thin obsidian knife.
I slip it easily beneath his ribs
and sew myself and my kind
to the heart of the continent.

We Left the Theater of the White Rose

We left the Theater
    of the White Rose,
laying down
    our heavy leather masks.

The bone moon
    rose from behind
bloodstained
    wads of cotton.

We saw then
    that the path to
the Black Glacier
    was blocked with whale bones.

We have forgotten
    our fathers' speech.
We live now
    at the front of our eyes.

Columbia River Suite

The Glacier

The poet's imagination
gives off a primeval light
and holds within itself a script
of buffalo bones and medicine bundles.

At one of its sources the river
is a field of ice
spilling into the Pacific.

At fourteen I was a passenger
on the S.S. *Alaska*—enroute to Seward.
We passed the glacier
from one mile out.
The captain slowed the ship,
and as his engineer blew the whistle
tall ice columns
splintered into the sea.

At thirty I'm traveling nowhere
except to work five days a week,
an irritable passenger, like the rest.
On its course down Market
the bus passes stores and offices
where windows of black ice
hold people frozen in postures of despair.

Today my lunchbox froze to my side
and I looked at my reflection
and the faces of the others
for a sign, an illumination, a flame —
some demonstration of love to loosen the ice.

The S.S. *Alaska* cuts dark water.
We pass a glacier of blue ice.
Standing on deck
I feel the glacier's cold breath:

I have been here before, another century,
a boy paddling a cedar canoe.
The old men have sent me out alone
to discover my spirit.
I have fasted and paddled for two days,
the canoe drawn north by a strong force,
like a salmon after a feathered lure.

When I find I am near Ice Mountain
hair freezes to my neck and my arms tighten.
But I face the mountain,
alert and still as a hunted animal,
sniffing the sharp air
and listening to the shift and snap of ice.

The spirit of the ice sees me
and sits in my mouth like a dead man's teeth.
Then Land Otter slides swiftly over the bow.
I feel his wet fur on my back
and he chews my hair.
Then he whispers a song in my ear
and hangs an amulet around my neck.

I tap the paddle against the canoe
and sing Ice Mountain my song.
As I sing I see my ancestors
writhing like larvae in the mountain's belly.

I am to be a singer!
I will return to my village
and make up songs
about the old age of the earth
and our swift journeys beneath the stars.

The Salmon Festival

1

At Celilo Falls the Columbia
broke to a lather of water and light,

and the salmon, shooting from pools and shelves,
flashed like silver reflectors.

That day I had a vision
that the salmon would be my totem.

I am lost now in a polluted slough,
seeking a channel to white water.

2

The old chief was buckskinned in white;
he had braided silver hair.
He filled the longhouse with light
as he blessed and praised the river.

The river has been dammed
and the old man is buried now.
I bow to his burial canoe—
praise the brightness of the prow.

3

In the longhouse
six men around a large drum
singing:
of silver white salmon
of flashing water
of glistening stones
of white nylon nets
of sharp-white gulls
of white cranes in mist
of small white flowers

and:
of the shell-white East
of the moon as a polished white shell
of the Original Path being crushed white shell

Listen!
the drum is calling the Ancient Ones
Their white moccasins glide on the path
They stand now on the far bank
in the wet grass
singing quietly to the salmon

Across from Celilo Falls

for Jim Scoggin

Above Goldendale we sat on a power relay tower
and sketched the fences and roads
that ran through ochre fields of stubble.
We drove away with the next year's harvest
shifting in our heads—
the grain flashing like hard kernels of light.

As the car whined into the gorge
salmon entered our blood,
searching for secret channels.
That night, driving home through ghostly sage
we felt them swimming upstream
to spawn millions of eggs in our hearts.

Across the river from the falls we ate lunch
on a flat, grassy bank. Beneath the grass
rock sank its shafts deeply in the riverbed
and we felt the river sliding past the rock,
the cold, abrasive water working it.
We lay in the grass, propped on our elbows,
drinking pop, smoking,
watching the river in the afternoon light.

When we found the glyphs of fish, deer and sun
on the nearby rocks, our foreheads were marked
with signs; our temples pulsed like drum skins
and we danced.
We danced and sang *The Dance of the White Deer.*

The Great White Father

Engineers
found the Great White Father dying,
caught in a fish ladder at the Dalles.
He wore a rubber mask
that disguised him as an Indian grandmother
and his last words were,
"I want to be loved!"

After two centuries massacring
salmon and buffalo on the dark river floor,
he had tried to swim to the light.

The Medicine Man summoned
to sing for the Great White Father's shadow
had a vision of it slipping down river
towards Portland
bloated with ears and testicles
and human hair.

A Gothic Tale from the Vietnam War

There is a TOP SECRET room in the White House
filled with the carcasses of horses, dogs, and snakes.
At midnight the President's "favorite darky"
entertains him with a *soft shoe.*
Then he unscrews the President's head
and wraps it gently in Saran Wrap.
Humming "Old Black Joe," he collects the heads
of the Vice President, the Secretary of State
and the Secretary of Defense
and then takes them to the secret room
to soak in a compost.
The heads, renewing themselves,
make noises like giant slugs.

Prosepoem in White

The Conestogas creak across the plains,
blazing the pure white of starched Puritan
collars. The Anglo-Saxon fathers sit
behind their laboring oxen, whistling
'Rinso White,' like innocent meadowlarks.
They will cover the land with corpses,
and the corpses with flakes of Ivory
Snow. America will have the whitest
wash. Even whiter, by God, than the
wings of Catholic angels.

At night, beneath the moon, the wagons
change into a ring of ghostly mushrooms.
The gills on their undersides, formed of
pale dollar bills, drop a poisonous
spore on the prairie grass. Buffalo and
grazing Indian ponies grow blisters on
their stomach linings and begin to vomit
blood.

The White House dome grows spongy and
viscous. Inside, General Grant
drinks whiskey and smokes a piece of human
gristle. President Nixon drinks a glass
of milk and orders ten thousand bottles
of smallpox virus dropped on Oklahoma.
Indian-i-zation is going just fine.

The Vice President is on his way to
Sunday school. He is dressed in a white
pinafore, a white hat and white buckle
shoes. He carries a new white Bible.
Inside, the pictures show John Wayne
as Jesus, dressed like a Green Beret.
In the background are the little
Asian children, exploding into blossoms
of white phosphorous.

Following The Blind Woman

Ballad of the Sea Witch

At midnight, when the sea was calm,
the sea witch sent for Bill.
Her messenger was a great black gull
that screeched on his window sill.

When Bill awoke he kissed his wife
and kissed his children three.
"I'll not be long, my loves. I'm going
out walking by the sea."

The wind blew up and snuffed the moon,
the path was lit with fire.
The sea witch sat in a scallop shell
playing a whalebone lyre.

"I've made us a bed of sweetest fern
and a crock of rarest tea.
And mermaids to sing the whole night long.
Come, Bill, and lie with me."

Pearls and seaweed she had in her hair.
Her eyes were green as the sea.
And while they loved young Bill forgot
his wife and children three.

"The morning's come, you lovely bitch,
my breakfast waits for me.
And my dear wife will box my ears
if I don't come presently."

The sea witch laughed a terrible laugh.
Her eyes grew dark as the sea.
"No mortal who has shared my bed
returns to his family."

At midnight, when the sea is calm,
the good wife weeps in vain
and the children shrink from a great black
gull that pecks at their window pane.

To a Salesgirl in Juarez

She stood in the cool shaft
of a gift shop doorway, her dress
morning glory blue against brown skin.
Her presence loosened the chrome yellow light
and the afternoon expanded, touching each man
in the plaza with the spaciousness
and destiny of a conquistador.

I travel with her still through personal deserts,
my water bag filled with the elixir of her smile,
for even the lizards are sick
of seeing the black, swollen tongues of poets.

Mojave

In a time of drought her name was River.
After a month of rain I name her Mojave.

She brushes my face with a hawk-wing fan
and offers a nipple crusted with black salt.

The flies have taught me how to mourn her;
cicadas the dry sound of loss.

Sentence follows sentence into the desert
where wind erases her scent and my words.

Memory of her neck and the mucus of thighs
lures me to the entrance of the magnetite mine.

It is blocked by windrows of lice;
termites foam in the dead timbers.

In the mine shaft Chemehuevi chant a death song
about white men who prospect for dark women.

Behind me Kelso Dune shrieks and booms her name
and its quartz crystals grind an ominous light.

Saida

Your body, turning lightly in bed,
is a lighted ship moving in a dark bay
and contains the mystery of night and distance.
As you dock, knocking softly against me,
my skin reflects your lights
and our talk becomes the estranged voices
of passengers.

Your body, turning lightly in bed,
is a white Arabian mare
wheeling in the desert night.
The small bells in your mane
fill the room with music.

Your body, turning lightly in bed,
glows in the moonlight like plankton.
Wherever I touch you there is a radiance—
as of a night swimmer in a phosphorescent sea.
Beneath your skin there shines another light,
a sea anemone whose interior
is the electric green of pool tables.

I enter you in search of the ocean floor,
a unicorn cutting his flesh on the coral.

Eve

1

It is as if the hand of God,
brushing over us in the night,
incised my skin and removed a rib.
On waking I find a roe in my arms;
red petals trickle from my wound
and a Persian angel is blowing a rib flute.

2

I wake in an unfamiliar garden.
Leaf, petal, vine, snail, stone
separate from the mist;
our bodies, twined together like vines, take form
as if being shaped from wet clay.
Your lips, your ear, your throat are still moist.
I kiss you, savoring the juices of creation.

3

It is as if I have been inhaling sacred leaves
and am oracle to the strange syllable of your name.
I chant in a foreign tongue a prophecy to myself:
Eve Eve Eve Eve Eve—
a subterranean sound, like an underground spring;
a distant rushing, as of a stellar wind.

4

A loved woman is turned earth receiving male rain:
the heat and smell of you penetrate my sleep.
I return, a butterfly emerging from the dark,
to a bed thick with corn blossoms and pollen.
O Eve. *White-Painted-Woman.*
Mother of corn and precious shell.

5

We have held each other briefly in time.
I wake to find you have gone,
the sea shell imprint of your ear on my shoulder.

6

Is each union of lovers
the opening and closing of an astral valve?
I send you this poem as a charm
against the closing of that valve;
that we do not become casualties,
drowned lovers washed up
on the bleak littorals of freeways.

Sequel

Though I repeated the proper words:
moon, wind, blood, bone, pollen,
and mixed strands of your hair,
your menstrual blood, my semen
and earth—the formula failed
to coerce you. But there is
still the solace of song.

Standing now on Goat Hill
in a circle I've drawn
with a bone; dressed in skins
and shaking a rattle
of dried deer hooves, I give
your name to the dark winds
of the American night.

Below, along Mission,
disconsolate men receive
your name in their sleep.
May it transform them briefly
as it has me; they wake
to step across doorsills
into fields of bright wheat.

Moonsong for Jere

You are Falarr, daughter of a druid.
The dark trees turn under the moon

watching you for a sign.
You lie on a crescent of sand,

your arms outstretched to east and west,
a stone disc burning on your forehead.

Your eyes are the blue of a Kiowa's knife blade
unsheathed in the moonlight.

The cuticles of your nails are small moons
swimming beneath my skin.

Fire is in the grizzly's eyes
and his paws rake honey from your sex.

A drop of semen
quivers between the horns of the moon.

Siren—Woman and Bird

In a small bed we tried the nights.
The sails were the violet of your pupils
and were scented with patchouli.
Your sex was a soft net
opening and closing in the tides
and I a drowned swimmer
brought up from the ocean floor
to where your fingers
pulled sea anemones from my spine
and my body bled
against the coral of your teeth.

Siren—woman and bird,
you have folded into yourself
in a sleep that excludes me.
My poems are fading charts,
useless for mapping the currents
that light your feet
and the hidden reefs
that explode in your hair.

We Were Each Alone

En estas soledades estuviste:
Paris es un desierto para la timidez de los recien llegados.

     —Enrique Lihn

We were each alone:
San Francisco is a desert to the shyness of love.
You sat in a rocking chair by the window,
wanting to die. The streetlight on the corner
shone on your face and bathrobe with the bluish-whiteness
of desert moonlight. I looked in your eyes
and the pupils were as wide as a Sahara night.
You weren't in the room, but were walking among ruins,
trailing a broken wing.

I followed you and came to the desert of my self,
where sand and sky blazed a harsh light.
I asked my shadow for a prophecy
and it vomited three black yolks.
At the oasis a headless statue of Eros
was bleeding in stagnant water.
I walk now among dying camels
carrying a photograph of your eyes.

For Linda

1

We rode towards the stars on a crest
of marble, gneiss and schist
and were caught in the cold sweeping searchlight of eternity

2

You were the Snow Queen and I was Borís
I fought the Russians in the snow with my large red hands
As they fell on my knife their blood froze into jewels

3

I came to you and you loved me, Scheherezade
your breasts smelling of musk
and the wind in the tents

4

I can't tell you anything of love
except that it is a young woman
picking the dry rose-colored madrone leaves from her hair.

Marian At Tassajara Springs

1

I remember your hair
spread out like black moss against the rock,

your skin tasting faintly sulphurous
from the mineral baths,

your laughter like a spring
swelling up

from the lime and chalk of your pelvis
and flowing out the white stones of your teeth.

I caught the small trout of your tongue
in my mouth.

2

It was October.
The Monarchs were dying,

falling through the air
like oak leaves

and landing on the rocks and stones
where they would rest,

slowly moving their faded
orange and black wings

as if they were trying to fan themselves
back into flame.

We talked of the certain end
of our season

as the crumpled ghosts of old lovers
floated past us on the water,

and of something waiting
in cities and in each of us

that is hostile to love
and to rocks in clear streams.

I will think of that day
and the wings of your shoulders

when the firestorm comes
and the wind

whips my shirt
to black ash and orange flame.

Chama, In Three Mountain Ranges

1

Now we separate
branch letting go of pine cone.
On Tamalpais there is darkness, mist
and silence.

2

Are there daisies on the mountain now
and will we meet there again—
you to open to me from a white blouse
the gold cores of your nipples?

3

If you return to the spot on the mountain
where we ate slices of pineapple and watermelon,
say hello to the black ants who sucked the sweet rinds
and watched us making love.

4

Woman of the mountains touch me again
with your feet and hair.
Let me smell the pollen on your fingertips
and eat the petals of wildflowers from your sex.

5

Your hair is as beautiful
as a black fern
preserved for eternity
deep in a mountain of ice.

6

The veins in your hand are the veins of a leaf
that is slowly changing to coal.
Someday your hand
will heat the roots of mountain flowers.

7

In certain moods you travel back through your father's seed—
to the pitiless sun of the Sierra Madres,
and your eyes harden into the obsidian eyes of carved serpents.
Then you would have my heart steaming on a sacrificial stone.

8

We made love in a sleeping bag beneath a full moon.
Now the moon is the upper jaw of a skull biting the dirt
and the road through the Los Padres
is a powder of finely ground bones.

9

A wild boar runs through the Los Padres
with your heart on his tusk.
Hopelessly I stuff dead leaves
in the wound beneath your breast.

10

I have been searching for you
in the snows of the Sangre de Cristo.
Though I lost you only yesterday
I have suddenly grown old and snowblind.

For A Lady Who Loves Schubert

After a week in Hell
we are suddenly driving a yellow Volvo
through the snow in New Mexico.

This is a fact—
I'm not writing a surrealist poem
for *Sixties* or *kayak*—

we have spent seven days in Hell
with a Zen monk
who is as mad as the Karamazovs,
and now we are moving at sixty miles an hour
through snow and light
or, if you choose,
at six hundred miles an hour
through the pages of an absurd novel.

It's a wonderful vacation:
we've brought our suffering with us.
Through sunglasses—great cthonic masks—
we stare tragically into the harsh light,
Oedipus and Medea
bleeding in the small orchestra
of a foreign car,
while outside a chorus of Penitentes
flagellate themselves in the snow.

To the poet's noble profile
you offer a story from *True Secrets*:
'HE ONLY WANTED ME NAKED.'
You give me so much pleasure
that I'm suddenly smacked with joy
and I ask you to pass me the Joy Stretchers.

You're a hard bitch
for a lady who loves Schubert.

A Hybrid Villanelle on a Line by Li Po

Drunk on the moon, a sage of dreams,
I offer the mountain a shot of bourbon
and I offer you a shot from the hip.

The last full moon I called you on the phone,
drunk on the moon, a sage of dreams,
and talked to a cloud your ear.

Tonight clouds move across the moon
and I write this poem by candlelight,
drunk on the moon, a sage of dreams.

Drunk on the moon, a sage of dreams
I pick up the phone to dial your hair
but the line is dead, the mouthpiece a crater.

Two moths have snuffed out in the candle flame.
Drunk on the moon, a sage of dreams,
my moth heart crackles in the lunar fire.

You are probably making love tonight,
giving your monk rice wine from the hip.
Drunk on the moon, a sage of dreams,
I piss a bloody stain in the moonwhite dust.

A Day of Scattered Rains

It is a day of scattered rains.
A wind, blowing from the direction
of the Sangre de Cristos,
carries the scents of wet cedar and juniper,
of damp earth and sand,
and mixes it with the perfumes
of blossoming apricot, cherry and peach.

A thousand miles and two months away
and I am still disturbed
by these metaphors of your skin.
Nose pores and heart
are overloaded with memories of your smell.
I have become a cloud
swollen with blossoms and moisture—
the pain of left-over love.

Take me, wind, over the mountains
and let me break open!

Following the Blind Woman

for Dian

I am in love with the blind woman.
I am in love with the snake-haired Isis.
She came to the tomb of Al-Barash.
I heard her tapping her gold staff.
I felt her shake the door in rage.
She opened the great stone door.
She lifted the black basalt lid with her hair.
Blind Isis kissed my dead mouth.
She offered me the twin cakes of her nipples.
She gave me black wine and white wine.
She gave me an iron mug of beer.
She gave me cheese from the North.
She gave me cheese from the South.
She sprinkled me with fragrant cedar oil.

I am in love with the blind woman.
She led me from the land of the dead.
She sprinkled white dust of ground alabaster.
She made a path of white dust for me.
She wrapped me in fresh linen for the journey.
She coated my eyes with copper paint.
She gave me a necklace of lapis lazuli.
She gave me heart-shaped ear pendants of turquoise.
She coated my penis with natron and bitumen.

I am in love with the blind woman.
I followed her to the lake of black fire.
She had prepared a stone boat for us.
She wove a sail of heron feathers.
The boat was towed by a thousand gold beetles.
The lake sang and rustled.
The shore burned a blinding white dust.
The snakes in her hair whispered my secret name.

I am in love with the blind woman.
I am in love with the goddess Isis.
I am in love with the women who saved me from death.

I am in love with the blind woman.
I licked the mucus from her eyes.
It tasted of milk and honey.
The gold disk in her horns blinded me.
I saw with new vision and clear sight.
The snakes in her hair sang to the dead.
The columns of dead followed us.
They walked on the lake of black fire.
They left footprints of burnished silver.

In San Francisco

Three Perspectives of San Francisco

from Sausalito

Is San Francisco at noon,
bright and flat against
a cerulean sky, a fresco
by Pierro della Francesca
or a projection of the Beautiful?
Sporting a florid shirt
the color of an infection,
a tourist is taking snapshots
from the boardwalk in Sausalito,
unaware his negatives are
of a sprawling white hospital.

from Oakland

Is San Francisco at noon
white as the walls of Jerusalem
or white as the bones of blacks
bleached in the African sun?
A stoned musician, stumbling from
a hotel doorway, knows:
as the sun fires his silver
plated alto he begins to blow—
white buildings are facades
concealing kennels
where white hounds
fatten on crates of doves.

from Alcatraz

San Francisco at noon
is Venus rising from the sea
in a rush of sexual foam
to taunt the caged
with her white beauty.
What these pariahs see,
their faces pressed
against the wire mesh,
is missing in the vision
of Botticelli—
a nimbus of black light
surrounding her white flesh.

Freeway

An infected vein
carrying filth to and from the city;

a funnel
draining a huge operating table.

Even the light here
is the color of pus.

All the late model cars
have tinted windows to shield the murderers

and the chrome is honed
to slash and carve.

And the city has drawn
a rubber curtain of shrubbery

to enclose the view
and muffle the screams.

A Wind Full of Light

A wind full of light,
of blossoms of the lime tree
and pomegranate tree
blows beneath Market.

The damned, their noses and ears
plugged with dollars,
do not smell it
or hear it.

Their feet are lifeless—
toes that were meant
to send down roots
to tap the wind;

to break from the husks
of shoes
and, in the madness of the dance,
create whirlpools
of light and blossoms.

In a Country of Warehouses

I dreamed
I was a stranger
in a country of warehouses
where the sun beat hard
against concrete slabs
and the doors
were as large
as cathedral doors

Inside
in darkness
men moved about slowly
like priests
among the pallets
of cocoa beans
stacked drums
of peanut oil
racks
of copper tubing

Some carried cargo hooks
that flashed
in their hands
like holy rings

I found the hooks
had several uses
There
in the harsh afternoon
workers
gutted me
like a chicken
to tear out
whatever it was
they feared

They found
a black jewel
and
an ovum

These
made them
furious

On Goat Hill Following Rain

for Donna, Gwen, and Teresa

Clear air has followed a week of rain.
The houses blaze like whitewashed barns.
There is a special light contained in things.
It's released from apples when you bite the skin
and is packed beneath the bark of white pine,
lighting up the millworker's hands.
If only the light would consider me,
shine on my face as if my skin were petals.

Depression

My mattress floats in an ocean of newspapers
through the eternal night of the fifty states.
On the ocean floor generals and editors
ride sharks through forests of sea anemones,
sabering Sioux and negroes and Vietnamese.

I try desperately to sleep, to dream—
anything to shut out the hissing sound
of limbs and heads as they bob to the surface
from fathomless layers of print.
Any moment I expect my daughters' heads.

After My Breakdown

After my breakdown
I tried Compōz.
I went back to Brylcream.
I joined the Dodge Rebellion
and the Pepsi Generation.
I flew the friendly skies of United.
I put a tiger in my tank.
I ate the Breakfast of Champions.

After my first relapse
I filled my cupboard with Wonderbread,
my icebox with the beer beer drinkers drink.
I packed into Marlboro country
sporting a fresh tattoo.
I arrested death and decay with Macleans.
I killed body odors with Jade East.
I fought despair #100 with Excedrin
and pain #200 with Anacin
and anxiety #600 with Contac.

After my second relapse I cured myself
with Gillette stainless steel blades.

The Other

1

He assigned me a name

2

He is always here, goddamn it,
taking fingerprints, voice prints, odor prints

3

After my daily interrogation
I turn and walk out the door
It is always a deathly still Sunday afternoon
in a city like San Jose

4

He is a river of broken mirrors
grinding slowly past
Each blazing fragment
carries an instant of my life

For a Still-born Niece

A thousand miles from you, sister,
I plunge my wrists in the ocean
until they are braceleted with salt.
Then I raise them to the sun
as beacons for the child's soul.

Astronauts

We forget
that before we fell into the world
we were all star sailors,
that our unformed shoulder blades
were spurts of flame,
that we moved at the speed of myth.

We forget
that we are all heroes,
that we circled the moon-bleak pelvis
of the primal mother
and splashed down in a sea of blood,
bringing to earth
miraculous charts
etched in the palms of our hands.

Lost Names

The hospitals are filled
with those who have lost their names,

who have gone traveling during sleep
and returned to find a strange face in the mirror.

This morning I woke up and discovered
my shoes were filled with blood

and that an ambulance was parked
beneath my window.

Frantically
I wrote my name a thousand times.

Language

The vowels say: mother, rose, sea, pubis,
   love, grass, death, tree, blood and song.
The consonants say: father, will, work, honor
   rocks, metal, beer, anger and the general's jaw.

Sometimes the two make love and form words,
   the vowels held tenderly in the arms of consonants
   or rolling off the bed in an orgiastic dance.

Their children are sentences
   and are simple, compound or complex.
The simple sentences stay on the farm.
The compound move to cities.
The complex are very neurotic, like Proust,
   and become artists, criminals and professors.

On the Death of Theodore Roethke

The papers say he died in a swimming pool,
but that's not the way that poets go.
A poet's exit is terrible: as his hour
approached the wind began to blow,
rattling the windows of his study.
Below the lake shuddered; fish went still.
Above the light soured like spoiled grapefruit.
He listened and heard the awful rupture
of petals and stems and a chorus of worms
singing in the compost. He laid down his pen
and went out, feeling the weight of his flesh,
sensing his time of singing was done,
he who had turned the world into honey.
And he moved through his garden like a heavy bee,
his dark suit gathering a bloody pollen.

Three for Robert Bly

1

In the silence of the snowy fields
I found the frozen body of the poet.
His fingers were frostbitten and black
where he had wrestled a glacier for his poems.

In the distance I could hear
the music of his beautiful lines
as they were ground deeper
in the glacial ice.

2

In Minnesota the barns are black
against the snow;
there is a muffled, sickening sound
of blows to the heads of cattle.

In barn doorways and lofts
men whose mission it is to clear the State
of everything personal or strange
glance at luminous watches.

Some wait for the poet to step out into the night air.
They will freeze his body in cross-hair sights,
and each rifle has an infrared device
for tracking souls in darkness and snow.

3

The poet dances in the silence of the snowy fields,
his clothes on fire with light from the snow,
his hair burning in the light of the Crab Nebula.

John Haines

Opens and shuts doors in stone.

Lopes down from a blue glacier,
head black against the sunset's orange fire,
dark mouth prophesying.

John. John the Baptist.
Grasshoppers and honey.
Shaman. Mad monk in seal fur.
Drinker of melted snow.

Gives songs to the wind.
Combs ferns with a bone.

Talking of Yeats.
Talking of John Clare.
Drinking rum from a mountain goat's horn.

An abcess in his tooth,
an edginess.

A voice with boulders in it, rumbling around.

His songs made of basalt
and owl's blood.

from

The Sangre De Cristo Mountain Poems

A Man's Life

The life of man is like a shadow-play
Which must in the end return to nothingness.

T'ao Ch'ien (365-427)

The grasses and wild asters
are waving in the wind.
The jays are flashes of blue flame
in the pine trees.

I have just finished a bowl of Quaker Oats
with fresh apricots and raisins
and am drinking green tea
on the cabin porch.

At 33 the poet T'ao Ch'ien
gave up the glitter of courtly life
and went into the mountains
seeking the *Tao.*

Same age
I have come to this log cabin
where the wind sounds as if
it hones off a hill of skulls,

and the creek across the road
is the sound of the *Way.*
My past is 33 shadows
thrown swiftly on a screen.

Bow Hunting for Rabbits

For Littlebird

1

Littlebird, you loaned me your bow,
a wood and fiberglass recurved *Bear*,
and six aluminum arrows.
Now loan me your eyes and your Rabbit Song.

2

This evening I wounded an anthill
that was sneaking through the field
and stopped when it smelled my approach.
The hill was a blond rabbit
that changed into a tower.
The sentinels sounded the alarm
and the warriors put on
their metallic red armor
to foam out and attack
the aluminum battering ram.
I withdrew it with an apology
and the walls of the tower healed.
I could hear the Queen deep underground
singing a rabbit song
in her chamber of inlaid gopher bones.

3

This afternoon you brought me a gift
of a *Groves* white fiberglass and wood
53 lb. recurved bow.
This evening I went hunting
and discovered the magic of the bow:
it summoned Persians from the mountains.

They came on white horses,
rustling through the gold light
of last summer's oak leaves.
They were dressed in white robes and turbans
and carried ivory tipped bows
and quivers of willow arrows
fletched with nightingale feathers.
On their horses' rumps
they packed blue deer.

4

Thunder
and the sudden calligraphy of birds
against grey clouds;
my boots wet from walking
through willow shoots
and fields of wild flowers.

5

Because I was out of meat
and had not seen any rabbits
I shot a thrush at 30 yards
with a broad-head arrow.

I was proud of my skill
until I approached the bird
and found it flapping in the dirt,
half its head torn off.

Apricot Tree

For Beverly Dahlen

1

Sitting on the cabin porch
watching the stars and drinking wine with a friend,
I am suddenly aware of the slow, black
gnarled fountain of the apricot tree.

2

Oh bluejay in the apricot tree
aren't you afraid your feathers will catch fire
and your eyes burn out
in those galaxies of red-orange suns?

3

In the rain
the leaves of the apricot tree
are turning dark green.

There is large thunder over the mountains
and the small thunder of apricots
on the cabin roof.

On A Dead Swallow

Here you are, grounded in road gravel,
that yesterday flashed in and out of eaves,
your orange breast flaring like a coal,
your tail two columns of blue smoke.

I witness the transmutation of fire
as your flight passes like a shadow
into the swarm of black ants
that move in frenzy over your feathers.

Now they are burrowing around the eye,
mining it like precious metal,
saving this gold disc until the last
to raise up gloriously from your bones.

At Jeannie's in El Rito

There are simple pleasures—
such as drawing water from a well
next to a field where eight goats
are grazing,
and an ancient Spanish goat man
forks alfalfa.

Sometimes

Sometimes there is as much anger
in loving as love.
Feeling blacker than fish guts
I leave her
for a walk in the early morning light,
and pick a torch of wildflowers
to cut through my hate.

Rito

Short for El Rito. The town dog,
ate handouts, everybody's friend
until deliberately run over by drunk teenagers;
then became Jeannie's, who picked him up,
large as he was, and took him home.

They cracked his spine, but not his spirit.

We brought him to my place in the mountains,
hoping he would heal.
Each day he dragged himself down to the creek
two hundred yards from the cabin—
and I always had to fetch him and carry him
back up, muddy and stinking.

He wouldn't be still; refused to be sick;
kept challenging dogs and horses.
The sores on his hind legs spread,
ate through hair and meat—
until they found bone.
Then we knew.

I dug him a shallow grave by the creek,
with my bare hands and a stick,
so that I could get closer to his death
(and his *life*) while Jeannie
fed him a last meal mixed with sleeping pills.
Then I carried him down and laid him in.

Shot him between the eyes with a .22—
and as his head jerked forward on his paws,
I swear, his soul rushed past me
and it dropped me to my knees, and my hat off,
and my tears were copious and hot

for Rito, the town dog—a free spirit!

Daddy Longlegs

Delicate as the skeleton
of an eight petalled flower,
it is trapped in the crevice
of a porcelain iceberg.

It fears death will come
either by cold and hunger
or by a sudden thawing of ice—
the flash and roar of water—

and it puts out tentatively
foot and foot and foot
looking for chinks
in the porcelain wall.

The shaman of the iceberg
observes the spider
from the toilet seat
and offers a White Owl cigar

as a reward for courage
then scoops it
to safety
on a *Saturday Review*

Trout Fishing in America
with William T. Wiley

Up above Boulder, Colorado:
Blue lupines in the rain,
Bell's red-orange salmon eggs;
A *Royal Commander* fly,
brown with white wings,
33 Rocky Mountain trout,
Potato salad
and 90 proof *A.M.S. Brand
Kentucky Corn Whiskey.*

Here's to ya, ole buddy!

Aspen Ranch Road

1

The light snow is silver on the road.
The moon is a cuticle of ice.
The rose hips are frozen drops of blood.
The stream falls coldly over the rocks.
All of nature clearly etched this morning.
Even my pain, which is as black
as the tire tracks cutting the snow.

2

The aspens and birches
are dying into themselves.
The buds are closed
like small fists.
This time of year
we grow harder too.
Our bones assert themselves
over the flesh.
They shine inside us
cold and white
as naked birches.

Kentucky

The major portion of the Kentucky poems are dedicated to James Still

October in Appalachia

The last katydid knocks its tambourine,
dancing me here into what dark dream?
A bloody cloth is wiped across the trees
and the hills are full of howling strays.

Coal trucks hauling tons of darkness run
from Quicksand and Hazard and Kingdom Come,
dragging huge roots on underground chains,
leaking inky water thick as caulking.

This rocky shoulder leans toward winter sun.
The delicate mosses pray, gripping stone,
and broken dulcimers break into flame.
The stars press our bones into what black seam?

Reading High School Poems
in Hindman, Kentucky

After exhaustion,
after days of talking *about* poetry,
hating my glib tongue and performer's mask,
I came across a student poem
that brought me to love again.

It was like returning from a journey
to find my house lit up,
fresh bread and coffee waiting
and a woman there standing by the chair
smiling and saying *welcome, welcome*
and *how was your trip?*

Then rubbing my shoulders while I ate.

Dog Dying

Dog dying in the hot sun.
Dog dying on a sheet of bloody leaves.
Crippled by car and dog fight,
rolled off the road shoulder to the creek.
Hind legs gnawed by muskrats,
wearing a seething mask of flies.

Dog dying, barking all night through my sleep,
barking for solace
against his bloody going,
a fever of maggots in his skull.

Dying there in the clear noon light,
the stink of him a smoke in the air.

We bathed him, we gave him water;
we should have leaned down to kiss his sores,
who reminded us of our fragility
and the mortality of nerves and meat.

On Campus in Kentucky

This huge maple lifts its rosy flame
among the red brick buildings.
Leaves sputter in the breeze,
spark and drift off.
I place my hands on the black, wet bole
and bleed into the bark.
The tree bleeds into the lines of my palms
and I am raised up in the hissing branches
above the Sunday traffic.
I can hear the atoms burning in the bricks,
rose-gray ashes drifting from cornices.

Shawhan, Kentucky: Winter 1978

The trees explode outward
in bursts of frost,
scattering crows across the snow
like black seeds.

Icy fog smolders
on the farm houses.
Icicles glitter and crack
on eaves and gutters.

Even so
the farmer across the road
has let out his sows
to forage the crusted fields.

These will have none
of my winter despair.
They plough their snouts
in the snow and fiercely live.

Western Kentucky Farmer

He soaks his calloused hands
in steaming hog's blood.
Talks of naked girls in the barn;
has written *and* published
a book of doggerel about God and Heaven.
Baits Julia and I,
his poet-guests at supper,
with a story about the time
he put a "nigger" in the firebox
between Chicago and Louisville—
"Didn't need a stick more firewood!"

60 years of hard labor:
fireman, mason, farmer and liar,
his face shoved up like an old boar's.
And *crafty eyed*—
delighting in himself and our discomfort
while his wife serves up,
winking at us conspiratorially,
dish after dish after dish
of the *finest* Kentucky home cooking

Dream During First Snowstorm

On this winter night a dream of Susan,
a dream of bird and tree and fire.
Cardinal, red as a gout of blood,
spread its wings and was turning,
turning, turning in a field of snow.

Then it was Susan, with unbound hair,
whirling in a scarlet nightgown.
As she danced the icy walnut trees
cracked open, each to its lava core.
The only sound was lava
hissing and spitting in the snow.

I woke, in the ashes of my sheets,
to a cold wind in the power lines.

Drinking With You at Johnny Angel's on Christmas Eve

For Christmas I wanted to bury my face in your manger.
I wanted to be wrapped in the swaddling of your hair,
annointed with kisses and sweat and mucus.
Instead you gave me a Gingerbread man,
who was tasty but sexless.

I knew your answer before I asked,
so I exited, covered with comic spittle.
Outside the stars were blowing on their knuckles
and a few angels were locked in androgynous embraces.

Back at my flat, three fools knocked on my door.
They had come from afar, following yonder star.
They all had my face.

For S. L.

In place of your neck
I have the bitter wind in my teeth.
I write your name in the window rime
with my fingernail.
The walls bleed an icy sweat
that mocks the sweats of love.
Armpit and genital moss
are frozen on the stones.
Moist cunt is iron mud
and the backroads eat my gut
like a tapeworm.

Driving, driving, driving
past the frozen spittle
of waterfalls,
wanting the fire of your hair.

No solace in other women,
and words, my trade,
lock their icy crystals
in the back of my head,
dig in my heart
like polar bacteria.

I have been exploring
this cold passion too long,
following it across
the infinite blue snows.

How the Jilted Lover Spends His Time

Reading, finally, *Madame Bovary*
and the *Tao of Physics*.
Pacing the floor.
Smoking Camels.
Listening to the traffic
and the trains and the wind.
Hearing words flake off the blackboard
in emergency classrooms.
Kneading balls of blood and shit
and throwing them at the calendar.
Avoiding sleep and its attendant dreams.
Searching for the lost dog of humor.
(Last seen bloating in the Kentucky River.)
Ironing my jester suit.
Writing the word *suicide* on the walls.
Mixing a glaze for my clay penis.
Looking at *Hustler* in the bathroom.
Shopping for Christmas presents
to celebrate the Christ child's death.
Writing mercury filled letters to my friends.
Broiling my heart in cosmic rays.
Sipping *Yellowstone* whiskey
in a bare limestone landscape.
Composing satiric, unfinished essays
on *Women and the Unconscious*.
Contaminating students
with phials of bubonic poetry.
Laughing hysterically
at the infantile bawl of 'Literary Careers.'
Waiting for the call that never comes
and for the dry bone of the telephone
to crumble off the wall.

Images from a Marine Landscape

Monterey

Snail

Today I followed your silver trail
from the back porch into the dawn.
At the beach I found your empty shell—
pale ear of the cosmos
listening to its own silence.

For the New Pup

Sobaka and I go outside
in the early morning
to check out an old pear tree.
It rotted and fell over
a long time ago,
but throws out new branches
and each branch presents
a hand's-breadth
of perfect white blossoms.

The grasses take part
in the morning ceremony.
One tall blade leans over
and drops
a shining water bead
on the pup's ear.

Lettuce

Tonight I slip from the house
and place my ear
to the dark earth
of our new garden.

I hear the secret life
of the lettuce seeds,
the creak of rigging
and the swelling of hulls.

Orders are shouted
and crates moved
as the precious cargo of phosphorous
is taken on.

I am waiting for the time
when I will find
green sails shaken out
beneath the starlight.

Beets

Today I'm depressed
with myself and the asphalt world.
I want to lie down in the garden
and become a beet.

I want my heart to be a dark root
swollen with rain water;
my head a green leaf
shot through with purple veins.

I want the secret, double life
the vegetable knows;
the joy of living
half in earth and half in air.

Crows

I love crows.
If I met one human size
I'd invite him into my living room
and offer him the softest chair.
Then we'd crack a fifth of *Old Human*
and talk late into the night.
The room would be filled
with the shine and rustle of his feathers
and the wit of his sharp eye.

Data

The dry sea of data
is rising.
A tide of newspaper,
ticker-tape,
carbon paper
and perforated cards
rustles at the edges
of our lives.

Each day
a passionate woman dies,
her flesh sucked dry
by the open mouth
of an envelope.
Or an angry man
of swollen lymph glands—
poisoned with fine needles
of paper fiber.

Two From the Monterey Hotel

1

Let's Raise a Glass of Port to the old Caddy

Didn't know much about the old guy.

>Face flushed the color of port,
>dressed in gold cap and wind-breaker.

Had a friendly word for you,
but stayed in his room most of the time,
cuddling his pint of Gallo.

>Remembering, maybe, the greens,
>the flags; breakers off Cypress Point.

And then they brought in the motorized carts . . .

>We found him recently dead.
>Fully dressed,
>curled up fetally on the bed,
>pool of brown vomit and mucus on the pillow.

His only angels a box of soda crackers
and a souring carton of milk.

>Had to help the coroner
>carry the stretcher down stairs.

Tibbits, a small man, but heavy in death,
weighing as much as two full golf bags.

2

Portrait of a Desk Clerk

She takes as long as a Kabuki actor making up,
fitting on first black lacquer wig,
then false eyelashes and violet nails.
Pats on cologne and baby powder
until the hallway has a sweetish stink.
While she elaborates her costume she hums,
merrily but tunelessly, *dee dee dum dum.*

She hums for me a few rooms down
painting over piss stains and despair with Fashion Tone.
She hums for the alcoholic down the hall
who thinks he is in love with her.
She hums for the whole third floor,
letting them know this dump won't get *her* down.

She's made up a story about an estate.
When it's settled, she'll be in the chips.
I nod when I hear it again, to help her believe it.
She's going to do something worldwide for kids
and will hire me at four bucks an hour.

With a final flourish of Lemon Mist
she signs out of her room
and descends the stairs to her estate.

Portola Cannery Poem

Bells ring furiously
summoning us on deck.
The boss's old sea turtle face
rises from deep water.
We are about to receive orders
to murder five million squid
for the gourmet tables
of the Greek dictator.
Already the bay is stained with ink.
Rusty gears, levers and chain-link belts
begin their slow grinding below.
I am ashamed of my part in this.
I throw my M-1 in the water.
I want to dive into the ink
and disappear forever,
like a drowned man
in a Medieval drawing.

Poem Against War

Two boys in a rowboat at El Estero Lake
are beating eight ducklings with a stick.
They do not know where to swim,
because the mother duck is frantic.
A man shouts at the boys from the lake edge.
They thumb their noses, stick out their tongues.
The man throws off his shirt and shoes
and begins wading and swimming.
But it's too late. The boys row off,
leaving the pulpy bodies in the water.
The mother cries, pecks at the bloody mess.
The man stands waist deep in the lake.
He is cursing and weeping.
This is how it feels to live in America.

Soledad

Driving to Class

1

Driving through the lettuce fields
of the Salinas Valley
I pass the pickets
of the United Farm Workers.

Red flags
stamped with the black Aztec eagle
snap in the wind
above flashing teeth
and raised brown fists.

Near Gonzales a crow
swings in a hangman's noose
from a telephone line.
It hexes the fields of a rich grower
who has bussed in scab labor
from Arizona.

A few miles further
the huge prison smokestack
points its yellow snout
at the horizon.

2

Eighty miles south, at Salmon Creek,
chaparral, oak, greasewood and pine
are exploding in the heat.
White ashes drift down on Monterey
and the sun is a diseased pink.

"It's as bad as the fire bombing
of Dresden," one man says.
The fire boss remarks,
"The hardest part is chasing
the burning animals back into the fire."

At Soledad the bureaucrats
flap wet shirts; the guards
drink beer and piss in the cells.
The burning prisoners fall back,
the world still safe from its crimes.

And where are you going teacher,
in your lettuce green suit and new cordovans?
Turn around, break into flame.
Leap from the car and run down the freeway,
scorched with the pains of birth and death.

Full Moon Over Soledad

The light of a full moon
falls on the prison.

Guards keep watch in the towers,
licking the oil from shotguns
with their lizard tongues.

Prisoners' hands reach out
of the barred windows,
thirsting for the pure
silver water of the moon.

Now and then a hand leaves
and flies away silently
like the wing of an owl.

Upstairs in the Education Wing

Upstairs in the Education Wing
we are rapping about the death
of *Psyche* in prison.
Each man is quiet, each thoughtful.
Tonight we are all together
and it is beautiful.

Toward the end of class
we hear shouts below.
The men are rioting in O-Wing again,
burning sheets and blankets,
sending up smoke signals from Hell.

After class,
walking the long corridor
of the Main Line, I pass O.
Through the small window
in the heavy metal door
I see guards in gas masks
and yellow slickers moving rapidly
through smoke and tear gas.

They are mutant locusts hurrying
to lay their eggs in the dead.

Elegy for George Jackson

1

They say you died in a patch of sunlight.
After ten lightless years.
Gunned down from behind.
Black man running through the woods
for two hundred years.
Gunned down in a patch of sunlight.
Gunned down by the sheriff.
Gunned down by the Ku Klux Klan.
Gunned down by the tower guard.
Gunned down while running through the alley
toward that patch of light,
that open space where you could breathe
at last.

I hope it's true
that you died in the sun,
that at least they aren't lying
about that.

Bless the grass that sponged your blood.
Bless the ant that drank from your tears.
Bless your mother's pillow
that has turned to a block of salt.

2

Perhaps you don't need these words
from a white man.
But I tape them to the wall anyway,
and stand in the shadows as you sprint by.
I am cheering you toward that patch of light.
This time you will make it.
Beyond the wall.
Beyond the fence.
To that open space that the sheriff can't see,
that the deputy can't see,
that the realtor can't see—
because the light is blinding
and the boundaries are intangible.

3

Your brothers are weeping, George.
This is the hour of lamentation.
This is the hour when the gun towers
turn into flaming pillars to mark your way,
and the barbed wire into guitar strings.
This is the hour of desire.
The worms are covering your skin with mica
in preparation for your ascension.
With Che and with Malcolm X
you enter the timeless hour of myth.

The Road to the Yellow Prison

1

"Are you going
to *Souldead* tonight"
said my woman's
little boy.
Yes.
To *Soul Dead*.
Along
the River Road
at dusk
in early spring
in the solitude
of a battered
'53 Ford
through
the lettuce capital
of the world.
To *Soul Dead*
a journey
that should be made
on foot
that should end
with me falling
on my knees
like Father Zossima
and kissing
a murderer's feet
because of what
I have learned
of suffering
there
without suffering
myself
because Americans
hide their sufferings

hide their deaths
in prisons
in mental institutions
in foreign wars
and they won't
fall down and weep
the cold blue eyed
Anglo Saxon bastards
Of whom
I
am one.

2

Soledad.
A Spanish word
for loneliness
for solitude
dark syllables
of the dreaming
earth
in the shadows
of the Pinnacles
a spot where
if there were
no prison there
a man might go
to speak to
his *Shadow Self.*

But the spirit
is twisted
in the House
of the Dead.

There a man
may not fall down
in the perfumed
grasses of spring
of mother earth
and nourish
his *Shadow Self*
his female self.
And looking for
the woman
in himself
he spills his semen
and his blood
on concrete.
He goes
insane
inside what is
called a
"Correctional
Training Facility."

3

After class
I get in
my sarcophagus—
my limestone coffin.
This is my
ship to the sun,
my stone boat
out of the
galaxy.

But it doesn't float.
Instead
it grates
up and down
the River Road
four nights
a week
towed by
twenty skeletons
hauling on ropes
of prisoner hair.

4

When friends
ask me how
I like teaching
at the prison
I open my mouth
and show
them a tongue
of sulphur yellow
dust
and two rows
of stone maggots
for teeth.

To a Wild Boar
in memory of Shunryu Suzuki, Roshi

To live like you, snout to the earth,
smelling the sweet pine needles
and the pungent tubers.

To plunge through a hail of acorns
and feel in the flash of my tusks
the lightning of the pure present!

Night: Soberanes Point

At the ocean my nose
was full of salt air.
Now on the path back
to the car I notice
the female scent of lilac
mixed with the male odors
of horsemint and sage.

As I lean over to break
a sprig of lilac
my flashlight finds
a Golden Poppy,
its petals folded
like a nesting yellow bird.

I switch off the light
and look up at the sky,
that dark unfolding flower
filled with rushing, burning
star anthers.

O blossoming night!

Robert Bly at Point Lobos

While I study the red blisters
of lichen on the dying cypress,
he scribbles furiously in the rain,
trying to capture the spirit
of rocks in a smoking sea
and the odor of wild lilac.

With his clear plastic raincoat
billowing like a fish bladder,
like a bag of waters,
I see him as he really is—
a stranger, risen among us
from a watery life.

Coast Live Oak

The oak is old
and arthritic
with gallnuts

Its limbs are bearded
with wisps of lichen

An ancient
bird's nest
rests on a bony branch

My hand
rests
on its gray skin

For man wants communion
across
the illusion of forms

There are no words
for how deeply
I love this tree

Yucca

Our Lord's Candle
bursts from the granite mountain.
Honeybees fling themselves
in and out of its sweet waxy flowers.

I climbed to it from a field of lupine,
a field of blue fire,
thinking no further beauty was possible
this spring morning on the trail.

And now this yucca seething with bees,
this harp cracking the mountain
with a continual hum.

Above Taugher's Cabin

The limestone ridge is mauve in the dusk.
The yucca's white waxy blossoms
rise from the rocks, tall as a man.
A breeze shakes their scent on the evening.

I sense a holiness here, a quickening.
Then I see the other blooms
flare up across the canyon,
like torches held high by unknown runners.

Working on Jeanne Inwood's House

Two hot days on a ditch
for a water line
with just a mattock—
fighting hard dirt
and rubbery roots.

This morning
the fog returns
giving the coast
the transitory appearance
found in paintings
of Chinese landscapes.

Even the ditch,
bristling with chopped roots,
has changed.
Each bundle of fibers
is dark with moisture
and tipped with a drop
of clear water.

California Poppy

Gold orange stoplight
in a vortex of blue bees

The hawk is smeared with pollen
and can't fly—
golden hawk with ruby eye

Mole looked at Poppy
and went blind

Ant stepped out of Instinct
and dozes on a petal

Sulphur ice
Orange lingerie
Butterfly furnace

To the President of the Company

that produces pop-top cans;
to the president of the corporation
that turns out plastic rings
for six packs
and the president of the conglomerate
that manufactures
disposable diapers—

give them each an eight foot gunnysack
and a stick with a nail on it;
make them walk this coast
in their suits and ties,
stabbing trash and stuffing sacks
until they trail behind
like bloated intestines.

Give them no mercy
but water and bread
and let a garbage truck
follow behind them
so they can empty the sacks
when they are full.

Yes, they may sleep at night,
but curled up on the roadbed
with only their gunnysacks for cover.

Give them no mercy.
Make them keep walking and picking
until their faces are sunburned,
until their expensive suits
are stained and ragged
and toes stick out of their shoes.

Let them walk the rest of their lives
in shame, hiding their faces from the stars.

Hiking the Little Sur

1

Early March.
Walking the Old Coast Road
to the Little Sur Trail.

A deep calm flows from the ferns.
I feel like an old carp
alone in a green pool.

2

Tired and in a dark mood,
hiking for a long time
in heavy redwood shadow.

But what freshness
in these small white flowers
splashing out of an old stump!

3

Up here on Pico Blanco,
bare limestone outcrop
beneath a three quarter moon.

I can see for miles
over the creased canyons.
A crazy, wild joy seizes me.

4

Except for wind through pines
is there a sweeter sound
than water over rocks?

The Little Sur wakes me up,
water pouring through
where lazy thoughts were.

5

The Little Sur is roaring white
from months of rain.
I lose the trail

and work along the bank,
picking my way over fallen logs
and massive boulders.

Come to an abandoned camp—
a torn black plastic lean-to,
benches made from split logs,

an empty gallon wine bottle
and dirty tin plates;
a tattered T-shirt

hangs sadly from a line.
White river, dark trees
I, too, pass on.

Bixby Creek

Frost

The air condenses
during the night

leaving a shine
on the ferns and grasses.

It's like silver pollen
glimmering in a dream.

When the sun flashes
over the ridge

I dance into my cold jeans
and step outside

to go for a walk
in a lake of pure light.

Alders

Growing in moist earth
by the creek,

pulling coolness down
into the canyon,

platinum in the early
morning,

silver
in the afternoon,

becoming then more
buoyant,

floating upwards on
the light,

flashing
in the wind,

making another music
counterpoint

to the flowing
of water.

At dusk the trees turn
inward,

listening to
themselves.

The saw-toothed leaves eat
darkness,

chew a wound in
the sky

and a deep violet oil
spreads downward.

It is then the alders
call me outside

to stand on the large
cabin porch

listening to the electric
charge of the night breeze,

the nearest alder tossing,
sighing,

like a body being swept
by dreams.

The Star Dance

The high stars hurt my chest
as they raise me from the porch
with piano wires and silver skewers.

Ghost quail drum their wings
on the moon's taut skin
and owls blow on bone flutes.

Below trout flash in the creek,
rising at drops of blood
that bead the water like salmon eggs.

Gathering Wood For Winter

The soft rasp of a bow saw
spilling dust on the horsemint.
Sweat, flies and this fallen tree;
the bitter oil of crushed nettles
and the living alders
breathing the morning light.

Back at the woodpile
milk foams around the steel wedge
and the halved logs startle
with their whiteness
like split loaves of fresh bread.

For the Alders Again

Each morning your branches
flung wide in welcome
to a friend you've known
for two million years.

Out getting wood again
I draw my bow across
the bones of your dead
and play saw music.

The morning light flashes
from leaf to leaf
from leaf to saw
and back to leaf.

I'm a blessed man.
I shine in a new skin of sweat
as I lift in my arms
your great spinal discs.

Going Up For The Mail

1

Walking up for the mail,
Sobaka in front of me
scattering quail,
snuffling the freshest holes.
Then he breaks through a beam
of deer scent, wheels
and splashes through again and again.
Each time he crosses the jet
he triggers a secret door
that only the deer know.
And it drives him crazy
because he can never find it.

2

A certain spot on the road
blisters with small volcanoes.
Black wasps simmer in the cores,
eyes and stingers lava-red.
They are so mad with life and fire
they erupt and fling out
to burn the world,
setting their first blaze
on Sobaka's ass.

I Would Like To Fall Down

I would like to fall down
in the road
and scratch dust over myself
like an old chicken.

There is pain in the syllables
Cesar Vallejo
and I repeat them over and over,
matching them with
the dark places in myself.

I wish my own name
were vinegar and oil
instead of
a rocking chair with hiccups.

Today I detest it
and the body that follows it around:
Old Bald Head,
Old Stubby Hands,
Old Vapid Eyes.

So I kneel down in the road
to test what it's like
to find the summer's first blackberry
winking back.
We have a good laugh.

Three Quail

Sluggish mind, no lines coming,
so it's out to the sleeping platform
and the morning sun.

Shirt off, propped on my elbow, reading
One Hundred Poems From The Chinese
when three quail

bob single file
through the tall grass
not ten yards away.

They are so fat and perky,
so intent on pecking insects,
that it makes me laugh.

Of course you know the sequel—
the poet hurrying to the shack
to bob over his notebook, like a fool.

Willow Finch

Can man love life enough,
little green and yellow
willow finch,
watching you snap up gnats
in the laurel by the window?

You bring to mind last winter
when a flock came
to my favorite alder
to peck the dry cones.

All that energy!
As if the leaves were suddenly
swept back into the tree.

Thinking About Suicide

The far cold stars above Big Sur,
the moon a cyanide tablet,
freezing the night to white crystal,
filling it with the odor of bitter almonds.
My shadow follows me down the road,
leaking from my boot heels like blood.

Winter Darkness

Rain and the roadbank
weeping red breccia.

Oak ashes flaking in the fireplace—
seconds of Eternity.

The termite is back,
scooping and grinding behind my eyes.

I pour slow shots of Jim Beam
in the rotten wood to wash him out.

Winter darkness comes early,
slashing across the cabin like a rock slab.

Sphinx Moth

written on the eve of Eric Barker's death

A moth the size of a hummingbird
that flew in last night
and filled our evening with shadows.

Hovering, feverish, beating now
against the glass. I study
the feathery hairs on its thorax,

the smoked eyes, the secret
pink underwing that wounds me
like an insane child's mouth.

I cup the moth's hot life in my hand,
open the window and give it
to the morning, to the bare alders,

to its destiny. It leaves behind
a fluttering pulse in my palm
and a silky smear from another life.

Death Is Behind Us

Death is behind us
with his brights on.
The inside of the car
is lit up like a poisonous flower.

The kids are fighting again.
An owl's bloody beak
chatters under the seat.

Carmen is weeping
because I have blunt fingers.
I'm crying because
I can't turn off the road.
Because I'm frozen in *Father*.

As I Listened on the Black Bone

As I listened on the black bone
I heard the crystals spinning
in the shadow man's throat.
He said, "Your life is not dark enough."
He said, "There will come a time
when poetry is the only clear water."
I studied my palm and tried to cry
but my throat was blocked with dust and ice.

Up on Bixby bridge,
that fragile eyebrow of sugar,
the Beautiful People
were filming a beer commercial.
The director looked right through me.
The actors smiled their aluminum smiles.
The cameraman pointed his laser at the surf,
where the shadow man lolled,
embracing a dead sea otter.

I pressed my hand furiously
on the edge of the mailbox.
"You bastards!" I yelled.
"Leave us alone!"
On the horizon Kohoutek
flared in the solar wind
and Bixby Creek
turned viscous with severed tongues.

Hornet's Nest

This huge bubble of chewed wood
hanging from a single twig
over Bixby Creek

This decapitated mummy head
wrapped in gray bandages
breathing yellow striped hornets

This death mask
with its soft buzzing song
its primordial tune

of instinct
makes me want to beat it
furiously with a stick

At the Sign of the Fish

The man with fish blood
streaming down his knuckles
kneels by the creek.
The rainbow, gold hook
tearing its gullet
vomits juices,
the stippled light
of its roses fading
with each heartbeat.

The light passes into the man
and hooks in his belly.
Anger comes up like bile
and mixes with
the salts of love.

He tilts his knife
at the evening sky,
wipes the crust of blood
and scales
on his pants,
stands in the creek, thinking,
waiting for darkness.

Spring Passage For Van Gogh

My heavy body walks
a flaming tunnel—
floating fire bushes
of purple lupine;
red coals of Indian Paintbrush;
Monkey Blossom's orange spurts;
fine white ash
of Queen Anne's Lace;
burning paste
of wild mustard;
white heat
at the morning glory's center.

My body finally free
of its heaviness,
passing through
the bridge's arched pelvis
to the ocean's wall
of blue burning pigment.

Prayer to a Young Gray Fox

For Joe Bruchac and an unknown woman driver

You made the night for Joe and me,
had run into the front tire of another car
and lay there stunned on the highway,
dark blood-flowers under your muzzle.

If all the beasts were gone, Chief Sealth said
in a letter to President Pierce,
men would die from great loneliness of spirit.

The driver, a woman, was kind enough to stop,
didn't know what to do, asked our help.
The three of us bent down to watch over you
in the great loneliness of the coast night.
Your gaze was so clear we couldn't speak.

Whatever happens to the beast also happens
to man. All things are connected. Whatever
befalls the earth befalls the sons of the earth.

We kept vigil, two sons and one daughter of earth,
decided you were shocked, had only a bloody nose;
helped you off the highway with thick gloves
to protect against your hunter's teeth.

We might understand if we knew what it was
that the white man dreams, what hopes he
describes to his children on long winter nights,
what visions he burns into their minds.

May you, fox, who runs through my dreams now,
your tail floating joyously above the chaparral,
carry in your memory three human faces
who loved you a December night.

Letter to Joe Bruchac in the Manner of Richard Hugo

Dear Joe: found finally my first copy
of *American Poetry Review*. Where else
but in our national cornucopia, the super-
market, source of everything from soup
to shrunken heads. The sheet's okay,
but nothing that set me on my ass.
The special section of Hugo's letters
did, however, provoke me to try the form,
though this feels, as his reads, like
prose with narrow margins. But on with it,
what the hell. "Sloth, like rust consumes
faster than labor wears; while the used
key is always bright," Poor Richard says.

On the coast and in the canyon we've had
one week of sun between two of soggy bread.
Most rain we've had this century, double
the average, paper says. The coast keeps
wanting to slide into the sea. Two weeks
ago a chunk of highway went, carrying
a heavy equipment driver to his death;
we've had our share of slides on
the old coast road, but no one hurt,
knock on wood. (Carmen dreams of death
by car and has a fear of heights.) At
Big Sur village, where the fire was last
summer and a big slide this fall, it looks
as if a huge plough has driven through.

But I wouldn't trade this coast,
this canyon, I love it so. I could go on
writing like Balzac twenty hours a day
and never nick its beauty; the wildflowers
are coming out already; lilac and rosemary
sweeten the air. Though I might have
liked another month of bare alders,
I can't complain that roots are pumping
out green leaves and polleny cones.
And Sunday at the creek mouth, at dusk,
three hawks were fighting in peach colored
light. The way they banked, rolled,
buffeted up and dropped made my blood sing.
Words are wanting then, whatever the season.

Haines writes from Anchorage, says they
may be starting a Poetry-in-the-Jails.
Great! Bring more poets in! Bring flowers,
women! Bring Whitman and Neruda. Bring
air and light. Paint the walls lemon and mauve.
Bring canaries and goldfish, racoon and deer.

Besides this crazy and practical advice
I promised I'd send him the second edition
of our *Words from the House of the Dead.*
And good luck on placing your novel.
Right now I've got to truck in to town
to see *Los Olvidados* in Carmen's Latin
American Writer's class. Keep some cold
beer in the box for when we meet again.
I'll do the same—Bill. 2-28-73.

Five Fractured Preludes for Blue Bear

1

Dear friend, I envy your fields of blue snow,
wolves singing at the edge of your farm,
moose horns black against the moon.
So I send you what winter news I have,
a few tracks across this paper's white field.

2

Our first winter storm today.
One hundred smoking mountains at the beach
and crackling glaciers of green ice.
Grandfather rocks coughing in their icy beards.
The brine on my lips is the salt of joy.

3

Sat in my pickup this morning
just listening to the rain on the cab,
inhaling the stew of bay leaves and mud.
That's all.
The dog kept looking at me.
He thought there was somewhere to go.

4

Borrowed a pack of smokes from the lady down the road.
Smoking and listening to Schubert
between the wild bars of music in the alders.
Franz Schubert died at thirty-one,
fatally in love with water and darkness.
Myself, I walk on surfaces, in too much light.

5

The Navajos swept down the plains
between the Rockies and the coast,
carrying the deadly arctic bow.
Sing for me their faces in the winter winds
and sing of your own boot tracks in the snow
next time you go out to milk the cow.

A Portrait of Blue Bear

There he is, folks, old Blue Bear,
crashing through the honey light,
pausing in his barley field
to raise up and sniff the air,
curse at his binder, swear at his tractor,
shout "Cocksuckers!" at the crows
covening in the birch tops;
growl joyously at the sun
glancing off the ice and scarps.

Yeah, ole Blue Bear, a hell of a guy
beneath all that gristle and grizzle,
a man who can't get enough dancing,
whose feet read 8 on the Richter Scale,
whose socks *alone* dropped in the Yellow River
would send Mao and his armies
backstroking furiously upstream.

Yessir, old griz loves Chinese poets
and Bacardi rum straight. And *restless*,
oh, *restless!* Always on the move,
can't stay out of his truck-lair,
back and forth between McBride and Dunster
bellowing rum-soaked poems at the Canuck moon,
belly rumbling at the fleeing stars
simply because he can't catch them.

Now you folks be listenin' for him,
my buddy, Blue Bear, snorting in his fields,
digging up his spuds with a broken banjo,
singing bass among the tenor coyotes.
Y'all listen and join him in a rousing version
of the *Whang Dang Do Ay Yippi Ay Yay.*

Watercress Motet

Countertenor	Watercress, sweet watercress
Tenor	Watercress, biting watercress
Tenor	Grows on stone, and in muddy recess
Tenor	Has small white flowers, does watercress
Baritone	And roots of soft light, wherein the trout rests
Tenor	Daylight gathers, like a sweet oil
Tenor	Daylight is pressed, like a sweet oil
Tenor	In the small white flowers of watercress
Baritone	And moonlight trails its silken hair
Countertenor	From rootlets of the watercress
Tenor	Crickets, snails and helgramites nest
Tenor	In the muddy boughs of the watercress
Baritone	In the wind shaken boughs of watercress
Countertenor	While burnished crayfish, unable to rest
Tenor	Glide moonstruck through its shadowy forests
Tenor	O the watercress calls the deer down
Baritone	O the summer heat drives the deer down
Countertenor	To dip their muzzles in the creek
Tenor	And drink and graze in the watercress
Tenor	In the underwater fields of cress
Baritone	Watercress, sweet water caress
Countertenor	We kneel at the creek to eat its white flower
Tenor	While insects sing to the Mother of Water
Tenor	And mica flickers in the sandy nave
Tenor	Of watercress, sweet water caress

Moonwatching and Steelhead

The moon rises over the ridge,
a chunk of milky quartz
set in a basalt sky.

Some nights the creek is dark wine.
Tonight it's clear gin
and I'm drunk on it.

Moonlight sifts down
through the salt crystals
in the cobalt waves.

It strikes steelhead
waiting at the creek mouth
for the winter rains.

They love the moonlight.
How they shine in it,
gills winking like hot coals.

A moonless night
weeks from now
I'll walk the creek,

my life glowing with their gift—
a thousand moons
shining from underwater stones.

Red Fly, Green Line

    Red fly, green line
swirling in the current.
Minutes of complete solitude
before full light.
    A silence
cold and clear as the water.

    Red fly, green line
on the creek's skin.
Morning rising like white powder,
pin-holes of light in the tree trunks,
    white juice
pumping in the grass blades,
small veins of light
    crackling
the granite, heating
mica and feldspar crystals.

    Red fly, green line.
The sun tips its hot pan
over the ridge, spilling molten ore,
    the canyon
in flame, burning
pink, yellow, orange, red
and my hands and face on fire.

    Red fly, green line.
The flyrod trembles
and a steelhead rises from the ripples,
    furiously
shakes the stinging fly;
walks on the water,
shedding white and silver roses,
eats my heart's red knot like roe.

A Week After The Storm

I try not to step on the young grass
standing straight up in the middle
of the road, as if surprised.

The rock walls have turned on
their mats of green light.

Small ferns have sprouted
like violin scrolls.
A cricket sleeps on one,
waiting for the evening concert.

The creek makes a pleased sound,
cleaning its silt on the new gravel.

Burls, gnarls, limbs and boards
litter the beach where the creek
cuts to the ocean.

The driftwood is changing color
from a wet dark to a dry rose.

The ground up stones and shells,
the salt in the air,
shimmer in the light.

Above, the coast highway,
with its worldly business,
arcs over the canyon.

This day will never come again!

Evening

Evening, and the canyon wall
taken with thimbleberry blossoms.
Each one five pointed
and the width of a child's palm,
the petals wrinkled and thin,
like crepe paper.

But death is here, too.
A bee hangs upside down
from a star
on the edge of the galaxy.
A white spider sucks out its life.

I put out my hand in benediction
and it glows in the creamy light.
I wait there as the canyon darkens,
as the yellow bee darkens
and the spider's abdomen
rises like the moon.

Winter Sea Light

A man and his dog
sit on a rock above the Pacific,
their faces masks of hammered silver.

On the horizon
the winter sea
lifts hills of burning salt.

Seascape

The cliff is crying
and my fingers are stained with red granite.
The dog tears across the sand
with a stick, breaking the tidal flutings.
Gray whales ploughing south for the winter
butt the rain clouds out of the way.
What great joy
in the rushing noise from their blowholes.
The plumes of light
rising from their massive heads
call us into the beaten egg white of the surf.

Water and Garden Images for My Lady

Fucking. Your lovely legs on my neck
and me inside you,
rooted deep as an icicle radish.
You cry out. You've lost your name
to darkness and violence.

But listen to the creek
gurgling past the bow
as we enter night's wide lake.
Trail your hands in the water,
where the lettuce floats
like green fire lanterns.

And the pea vines, Carmen,
that scroll the chicken wire,
are guitar chords across the lake.
All in harmony
for you.

Reading Reverdy, Reading Eluard

The cabin door open
winnowing the light
like a transparent wing.

The book of poems
open on the bed.

The last flicker in the world
pecks out its own heart.

A Nazi watches from the ridge,
spits in his leather glove,
gives the gunner a reading.

Someone has thrown a dead girl
on the porch. Her left breast
is pierced with a glass arrow.
Crushed snail shells
glitter on her Venus mound.

I write the word *freedom*
in my notebook.
I carve it in willow bark.
I kiss the dead girl's hair.

The morning paper says
an oil company has found
a blind Indian
wandering the Brooks Range
guided by a three legged fox.

They do not understand the augury.

Seeds burrow frantically
in our garden, scratching *freedom*
on roots, etching it in rocks.

At the beach I find the word *Man*
traced in the sand
next to a cake of bloody yeast
bubbling on a hot stone.

I pack my bags with the same old
poetry scripts
and board the Coast Starlight
with Pierre and Paul.

We are being exiled.

But we have the last laugh.
Paul has smuggled out the flicker's heart
in a little silver case.

*This section is for Jack and LaVon Curtis
and for William Webb*

Egg Ranch

Praise these hens, that pass from laying
our breakfast into chicken soup.

Three to a cage, too crowded to squat,
their single ecstasy is eating.

Their combs flame only when the hired hand
walks down the cage rows with grain.

White ashes rustle and spit then,
battering the wire, and he is an angel,

the Mexican, trailing a blur of wings,
unaware of his own glory.

Praise these, whose shit we shovel into the pickup
to quicken my neighbor's trees.

Not theirs darkness and warmth of the henhouse,
but to stand all night beneath naked bulbs

going crazier and crazier, dropping suns
and moons into the harsh hands of men.

Big Sur: December: Drought

1

Icy half melon of a moon
spill your sexual juice
on the road's white dust.

2

The bluejay cries sound more and more
like prying loose old boards.
And the grey squirrel barks its complaints
that the acorns this year are dry and bitter.

3

Woke up this December morning
at that still moment before dawn,
after dreaming a violent river. And women.
Another day of sun and granitic dust.
How often my life
has been a dry riverbed.

Running

Breathe in lupine, breathe out lupine.
Man and dog running the road's parched lung.

My eyes inhale the purple flowers
and swish them around in the skull—
an afternoon cocktail.

Water and fire the petals,
water and fire the heart.

Neither Jesus nor Marx; not Buddha
nor astronauts from distant stars—
but something breathes us.

Some thing.

Breathes the dog and me and lupine
and the road and this imploding
and exploding heart of deerflies.

Sleeping Out

The swollen moon spilled into my sleep
and the silvered road dust sang.
The dog and I got up and went for a walk,
to see if the deer were dreaming.

Crickets shrilled in the moonburst thistles
and ancient sycamore hulks floated on the sky.
On the road we met Li Po
searching for one of his lost poems.

He offered me a bowl of rice wine
and we toasted, we toasted the moon.

On Reading Stafford's
Stories That Could Be True

Bill, it's a full moon tonight,
which means the shadows are deeper.
I'm thinking about you as I test them
because your poems say you are a man
who wades in shadows up to your neck.

If we lived former lives
I'd guess you were a tree—
a cedar, pine or oak.
You were a listener then, too,
holding the wind and moon in your branches.

The Buddhists talk about Original Mind,
a country we should find our way back to.
You seem to know that path by smell
and how the loose stones and bruised grasses feel.
Even the dust in your boot soles is wise.

Three Short Takes

1. Those Crows

   Those crows
   rattling the dry sycamore leaves
   are the day's street sweepers.

   They pick at the confetti of feathers,
   mouse tails and other trash
   scattered by Mr. Owl and Mrs. Fox.

   One ragged fellow
   in the top of a tree
   smokes the cigar butt of the sun.

2. Deer in Drought

   50 deer under one oak
   driven there by the puma sun.
   Browsing the ashen grasses,
   waiting for thin acorn rain.

3. An Image of Drought

   The sun
   is a cabinet maker's
   gold stained finger
   rubbing the color ochre
   into the grain of things.

Milling Redwood Up Vicente Creek

We rise out of the old sawdust, like ghosts,
our hands bloody with redwood stain.

Gouts of fresh sawdust wash over us
from the pink-gold heart of the new log.

We jabber and joke and tease,
exhuberant at each true 4×8.

Frank, John, Robbie, Sam, Bill—
a brotherhood of men in honest labor,

dancing, as earth lurches around the sun,
to the vortices of knots; the nebulae of grain.

Cities of Assassination

April Night

For Dian

The full moon is a blue rosebud
and the stars are distant chimes.
There is the rustle of bird wings
in the eaves, flame roaring in the wood stove.
Our daughters are dreaming
and you perhaps are dreaming, pregnant lady.

But I am awake, sipping coffee,
warming my butt at the stove,
studying your watercolor of Acacia
as "Spiderman"—
a terrified child swinging through the void.

And Amber, now in her fourth month,
fist sized, rocking in the amniotic fluid,
her face, like your paintings, unfinished
but taking form with each heartbeat
and the lightnings
that flicker across the umbilical.

I stare at your painting
and the terror in Acacia's face.
I think about all the sleeping faces,
and about Whitman's poem
on the dead Union soldiers,
their faces peaceful beneath the moonlight.

Oh at birth head and face push forward first
like a bowsprit into waves of light!

Two from Rancho Cieneguilla

for James McGrath

Morning

The bird tracks in the dust
greet me as I jog down the road.
The green lichens and the orange lichens
on the basalt ridge have awakened
and shoot out bands of light.
The petroglyphs make a clicking noise
as they brush their teeth.
In the orchards I hear the plums sweetening,
and the grass is ripe with pears and apples
that lie about like fallen drumbeats.

Hummingbird is awake early, too,
blowing and sucking on the wildflowers
like Kokoapelli.
And oh, yes, Butterfly is not to be outdone—
she dances and leaps from sunflower to sunflower,
shaking out her black and orange silks.

Night

We have come for dream time.
We have come to let the rock figures guide us.
We hear them whispering and singing in the dark.
Snake and Lightning watch over us.
Lizard, Frog and Beetle bless our sleep.
Holy Man raises his arms to the Sun Father,
whose black light shines on our sleeping faces.

We dream, we weep, we are overcome by so much love
pouring down on us from the basalt ridge.
When we wake up we feel cleansed and healed.
We are filled with new power.
We come out of our tents to meet the day,
bearing new shields and lightning-tipped lances.

Written at Michael Good, Fine Books

in afternoon light, San Anselmo, California,
January 28th, 1982, the Year of the Dog.
Gross Morbid Anatomy of the Brain in the Insane
open on the desk. by I. W. Blackman, Pathologist
to the Government Hospital for the Insane,
Washington, D.C. 1908.

Blown magnolia tree at the window.
Pink flame of the tulip blossoms.
Plate XXVI, Autopsy No. 1969, Case 11960:
B.W.; aged 60; male; white; soldier; nativity, Kentucky.
Mental disease, chronic epileptic dementia.
B.W.'s brain flayed open, showing effects
of hemorrhage, raw bleeding, gross morbid anatomy of . . .

1982, the Year of the Dog. B.W., age 46, nativity,
Missouri. Brain showing effects
of Gross Morbid Anatomy of an entire culture.
Wired on sugar, hooked into the flickering phantasms
of news and soaps; images of gratuitous violence.

1982. The Year of the Dogs.
Dogs wild in the streets. Plutonium in the rivers.
The decade of Book Burning
and why Johnny *won't* read.
Fantasy Moguls filming in the crypts,
the hacks hacking, hemorrhaging over their scripts.

Pink and white flames of the tulip blossoms.
Book husks heating the room.
The fire of words, breath and flame.
Bring us back to the body.
Bring us back to books.

Sobaka in the Underworld

My cigar smells like a wet dog.
Outside night rain tars the street—
a glistening road to the underworld.
I put him to death,
who loved me nine years;
who sat with me all day in the pickup
studying my face as I studied the bridge.

Dog-child and Man-dog,
I am dry eyed in the Crisis Ward
fearing my daughter's birth,
beaten with the metal leash of the Logos.
"Oh, master, I've served you
all my life."

We love dogs
because we've lost our bodies.
Logos split us.
No matter how often we copulate,
we are destined to wander
looking for our hands and faces.

Earth, forgive me—
my guide through wet fields,
leaper and tearer at the beach—
I gave him a quick needle.

Dreamed him again last night,
old farter and itcher,
shaking off the dark river,
wondering where we might go next.

Amber & Acacia, Reagan & Gorbachev By Starlight

Acacia grouses
because she *hates* sleeping out.
"The cats will get us!
Ants will crawl on us!"

And even outside,
drenched in night's beauty,
Amber has her *clock* nightmare.

We four watch
the *Kachina*-clouds go home,
leaving a vast, dark, crystal bowl.

The girls drift away to sleep.
A few stars, who want more light,
lean down to browse their blonde hair.

Stars, be kind to them
and to all sleeping children.
Let them live out their time.

Distill poetry and corrosive dew
in each and every missile silo.
Leak into the White House

and the Kremlin; secrete music
in Reagan's and Gorbachev's shoes—
that they might wake to a different dance.

Water Striders on Paper Mill Creek

after a lithograph by Richard Lang

Do they delight
in being lighter than water,
or is their only grace
that of predators?

Once I saw an emerald hopper
vault the creek and miss.
Oh, the water striders danced
then on their wet web,

came swiftly striding
on telegraph stilts
to cover the carapace
with living hair.

When they had finished
their gravy and meat
they picked their teeth,
told a few jokes

and then went dutifully back
to walking the surface tension
between fish and bird,
between shadow and sun.

Irises

Mike and Sandy
this is just to say
the dirt loves us.
Opened the kitchen curtain
for light
and was shaken awake
by your purple and yellow irises—
swollen and dripping color
on the morning canvas.

Iris, messenger from the gods
and goddess of the rainbow.
Beauty, dressed in her classic
and romantic robes,
or just pure flower, nameless.

And I, who have grown older
and more cynical
toward such invocations,
was already at work on another poem,
slurping a cup and musing.

This is just to say
no matter how much in debt
or how miserably we primates
treat each other,
the earth loves us.

This morning I pulled
the curtain on your garden
and a rainbow
arced into my coffee cup.

Three Travel Poems

1

Driving the Palouse in a Blue Mustang
with a pack full of mixed metaphors

The rolling hills lift plankton,
young emerald wheat
and disked umber clods of earth.

Bleached ranchers in baseball caps
whip by in pickups,
while a black and white magpie
feeds and lifts, feeds and lifts
in the fire of a mashed pheasant.

Around a curve
so much depends upon a yellow tractor
casting its net at the stars.

2

Lunch in the Park Cafe, Vancouver, B.C.

All the men conserved in suits—
tweeds, plaids; most wear ties.
Even here the warp and woof of money.
Two secretaries talking shop
over sherry and dessert.

Aida dropped me downtown
on her way to work at Provincial Health.
"Most old people hoard their money," she said.
"To insulate themselves against death," I said.

My waitress is regal—
black slacks, white blouse,
pulled back night hair
in which I'd like to sleep forever.
Her image multiplied in mirrors.

Regan her name.
Half East Indian, half English.
One of Lear's sour daughters.

I am in love,
but am left with dessert and little hope.
Over coffee I ponder Lear on the heath,
kingdom and gold scattered.
Executive suit in tatters,
tie hissing in the wind like a snake.
The whole continent thrown away.

3

Amtrak: 27 March 1984. 2 a.m.

We beat up on the forests,
beat up on the whales,
beating up now on the primal *selva*.

Passing small towns
on the same train
that beat up on *les sauvages*.

This travelling shooting gallery
dinging tin buffaloes
with Winchesters, with Smith & Wessons.

Wheels click off:
wood, wax, whale oil, petrol.

Electric towns leap from darkness,
cemeteries of asphalt and stucco—
glass embers of a dying star—
streets, lives
fleeting as this train
rocking through the Western night.

To Bixby Creek Again,
And To You, Raccoon

Shocked awake
by the half-nail moon
jabbing deep into the canyon.
So bright I felt
an unnamed guilt in my gut.

Fell back to sleep
as the moon traced the sky.
Woke again near dawn
to your perfect footprint
on the misted window—
like burning lace.

Thanks, masked partner
and fellow poet
for sharing in the night's crime,
whatever it was.

And let's not
let those bastards catch us.

Working Class Haiku

Scorpion shadow
of the backhoe falls
on a ditch deep as my grave.

Tu Fu Writes Li Po
From Cerro Alto Camp

1

Dear Kevin: you asked me to respond
to your poems. I am, then, moved
to my former style by your musick;
your Elizabethan sweetness; your lines
all lutes and viols. There are
flaws, excessive notes here and there,
an adjective or two awry,
but you will shuck them with age
and get closer to the bone.

When I woke up this morning
to the frosted dime moon,
I knew I had come home again;
who left these mountains
five years ago for fatherhood,
for madness, for cities, for politics.

Woke up numb and chilled
to, as I say, the sliding winter moon.
To a wind in the firs
and two yearlings feeding,
high stepping the dry grasses,
nuzzling bark and ferns.
We three stared at each other
in the morning stillness
and I was stirred
to the moral aspect of naming.

What you and I and Hannon know
won't show up on our job applications:
that the poem—Mind-at-Large—
spends our whole lives writing us,
and that the poet's calling
is always to be there,

to have the courage to stand all night,
if need be, beneath a feminine sycamore
to divine the tree's dreaming.

2

One man and two yearlings.
Three poets on the same path
we walked last Sunday.
Path to where, it doesn't matter.
I walked it again this morning,
past that perfect rock in that perfect pool
where we three stopped in silence.

Today
a congress of water striders
were flicking the morning ripples
on and off, systole and diastole,
pulse and convulse of life.

Walked further on the mulched path,
the bronze and rose leaves
warming my boots. Climbed past
the blood-spattered toyons
to where the ocean fog boiled
over the ridge, and stopped there,
facing a hillside of scree
and skeletal yucca.
Yet even in death these gray cocks
burst from their spikey fur
and dry pods thrummed in the wind.

3

Friend, keep writing poems
and send me some news in the mail.
I know a brother when I meet one.

August 6, 1914

Sexual Beings
landed on the Plains of Death.
The Life Pod tumbled
through volcanic winds and fires
and split open.

They walked out bravely—
naked, innocent and shining.
The males touched rocks
with their penises and trees sprouted.
The females put stones in their vaginas
and made a rich soup of words.
Birds began singing in their hair.

God saw that it was good.

But on the Plains of Death
they quickly covered their nakedness.
They were encircled
by ranks of Iron Knights,
horses and riders cinched in black mail.

Yet the Sexual Beings had courage.
They walked forward chanting,
offering gourds of pollen and wine.
The women crooned, "Feel my nipples
and stroke my hair, O knights."

This was God's joke.

"My liege!" shouted the knights as one,
and raised their lances for the kill.

The Lamb Of Peace,
The Ram Of War

Barbarians sweep down from the Carpathians,
iron helmets casting sharp shadows.
Swordsmen disembowel the moon
and raise up Christ and Lenin
in rituals of lightning and sperm.

Blitzkrieg: warriors smear their foreheads
and lintels with vaginal blood,
their spear tips with uranium.
They build cities of assassination
at the mouth of every river.

Liars, murderers, thugs—
they appoint Yahweh head of CIA,
implant tracking devices in foetuses.
Rasputin drops his pants at dinner,
says, "*This* is the Tsar of Mother Russia!"

Are you washed in the blood of the ram?

The lamb, the calf and the wolf cub
lie down together, panting,
waiting for the skies to heal;
wary of the missile phalanxes
flashing above the trampled wheat.

Within the cities of assassination
blinded children
try crayon drawings of the moon.

from I Go Dreaming Roads

by Antonio Machado

Carmen Scholis
William Witherup, translators

A Note on Translation

Translating a selection of poems from the Spanish poet, Antonio Machado, with Carmen Scholis, who did the hardest part of the job, had a profound effect on my own life and composing. When two poets meet in the process of translation, the poet being translated, especially when it is a poet of Machado's depth, passes on something of his or her soul.

I have never been to Spain, but Machado took me there. To repay the favor, I invited him to our cabin in Bixby Canyon. He came, and we spent many a fine evening discussing poetry over glasses of red wine.

Of the three Spanish language poets I have co-translated— Vicente Huidobro and Enrique Lihn are the other two— Machado is the closest to my spirit and the major influence on my Bixby Creek pastorals. This is the reason I claim these poems as partly my own and why I have included them in my Collected Poems.

Yo voy soñando caminos

I go dreaming roads
of the afternoon. The golden
hills, the green pines,
the dusty oaks! . .

Where will the road go?
I go singing, traveler
along the footpath . . .
—the afternoon is falling—.
"I had the thorn of passion
in my heart;
I managed to pull it out one day:
I no longer feel my heart."

And the whole field remains
a moment, dark and mute,
meditating. The wind sounds
in the poplars by the river.

The afternoon grows darker;
and the winding road
turns faintly white,
grows obscure and vanishes.

My singing returns to lamenting:
"Sharp golden thorn,
who could feel you
nailed in his heart."

Cante Hondo

I was meditating, absorbed, winding
the threads of boredom and sadness,
when I heard
through the window of my room, open

to a warm summer night,
the wailing of a lazy ballad,
broken by the somber tremolos
of my land's magic musicians.

. . . And it was Love, like a red flame . . .
—A nervous hand put a long golden sigh
on the vibrating string,
which was changed to a fountain of stars—.

. . . And it was Death, the knife in the shoulder,
the long pass, grim and skeletal.
—So I dreamed it when I was a child—

And on the guitar, resonant and trembling,
the brusque hand, striking, mimicked
the blow of a coffin on the earth.

And it was a lonely weeping, a breath
the dust sweeps away and the ash expels.

Es una forma juvenil que un día

A youthful figure comes
to our place one day.
We ask her: "Why do you return
to the old house?"
She opens the window, and the whole countryside
of light and smell drifts in.
On the white path
the tree trunks are turning black;
the topmost leaves
are green smoke dreaming in the distance.
The broad river
seems like a lagoon in the white
morning haze. Through the violet mountains
another chimera is walking.

Abril florecía

April blossomed
before my window.
I saw two sisters
among the jasmine
and the white roses
of a flowered balcony.
The younger was sewing;
the older spinning . . .
Among the jasmine
and the white roses
the smallest,
rosy and smiling—
looking toward my window.

The older kept turning,
silent and pale,
the spindle on its staff,
winding the flax.
April blossomed
before my window.

One clear afternoon
the older was crying
among the jasmine
and the white roses
and in front of the white flax
she threaded on the distaff.

"What's wrong," I said,
"pale and silent girl?"
She pointed to the dress
that her sister began.
The needle shone
in the black tunic;
the silver thimble
on the white veil.

She pointed out
the sleeping April afternoon,
while the bells were heard ringing.
And in the clear afternoon
she showed me her tears . . .
April blossomed
before my window.

It was another bright April
and another lazy afternoon.
The flowered balcony
was deserted . . .
Not the little one
smiling and rosy,
nor the sad sister,
silent and pale,
not the black tunic
nor the white veil . . .
The flax was turning
by an invisible hand,
all alone on the spindle,
and in the dark room
the moon of the clean
mirror shone . . .
Among the jasmine
and the white roses
of the flowered balcony
I looked at myself
in the clear moon of the mirror
which dreamed far away.
April blossomed
before my window.

Campo

The afternoon is dying
like a lowly hearth burning out.

There on the mountains
a few embers remain.

And the broken tree on the white road
makes you weep for pity.

Two branches on the wounded trunk, and one
stained black leaf on each branch!

Are you crying? . . . Between the golden poplars,
in the distance, love's darkness waits for you.

A Juan Ramón Jiménez

for his book *Arias tristes*

It was a May night,
blue and quiet.
The full moon shone
above the cypress,

lighting up the fountain
where the spouting water
sobbed intermittently.
Only the fountain in the silence.

Later the accent
of a dark nightingale.
A gust of wind broke
the fountain's arc.

And a sweet melody
wandered over the whole garden;
a musician played his violin
among the myrtles.

It was a sad tune
of youth and love
for the moon and the wind,
the water and the nightingale.

"The garden has a fountain
and the fountain a chimera . . ."
Sang an aching voice,
soul of the springtime.

Voice and violin grew silent,
muffling their melody.
The melancholy remained
wandering over the garden.
Only the fountain in the silence.

Canciones de tierras altas

I

Through the white mountains . . .
The light snow
and the wind in your face.

Among the pines . . .
The road being erased
by white snow.

Strong wind blows
from Urbion to Moncayo.
High barren plains of Soria!

II

Now there will be storks in the sun,
as I look at the red evening
between Moncayo and Urbion.

III

The door opened that has
hinges in my heart,
and again the gallery
of my story appeared.

Again the small plaza
with blooming acacias,
and again the clear fountain
telling a poem of love.

IV

The brown oak
and the stone desert.
When the sun sinks behind the mountains
the river wakes up.

Oh distant mountains
of mallow and violet!
Only the river sounds
in the darkening air.

Moon turning purple
in a late evening,
in a cold field,
more moon than earth.

V

Soria of blue mountains
and violet deserts,
how many times have I dreamed of you
in this flowered plain
where the Guadalquivir
flows to the sea
between golden oranges!

VI

How many times did you blot out
these green lemon trees
with shadow from your oaks,
land of ash!

Oh fields of God,
between Urbión and Castile
and Moncayo and Aragón!

VII

In Córdoba, the mountaineer,
in Seville, the sailor
and deckhand, who has
his full sail to the sea;
where the sand sucks up
spittle from the bitter sea,
toward the Duero's fountain
my heart returned,
pure Soria . . . Oh frontier
between the earth and the moon!

High bleak country
where the young Duero flows
land where home is!

VIII

The river wakes up.
In the dark air
only the river sounds.

Oh bitter song
of water on stone!
. . . Toward the high Hawthorn
beneath the stars.

Only the river sounds
in the valley's depths
beneath the high Hawthorn.

IX

In the middle of the field
the vacant hermitage
has its window open.

A greenish top.
Four white walls.

In the distance the stones
dazzle in the rough Guadarrama.
Shining, soundless water.

In the clear air
the thicket's small, leafless
poplars, March lyres.

En memoria de Abel Martín

While the fiery fish draws its arc
beside the cypress, beneath the richest indigo
and the blind boy of white stone rises in the air,
and the ivory song of the green locust
throbs and vibrates in the elm,
let us praise the Lord—
the black stamp of his kind hand—
who has commanded silence amid the clamor.

To the God of distance and absence,
of the anchor in the sea, the full sea . . .
He frees us from the world . . . He's present, everywhere—
and opens paths for us to walk.

With a cup overflowing with shadow,
with this never filled heart,
let us praise the Lord who made Nothingness
and has carved our reason out of faith.

Tu poeta

Your poet
thinks of you. The distance
is lemon and violet,
the countryside still green.
You come with me, Guiomar.
The day goes from oak grove
to oak grove, wearing itself out.
The train devours and devours
day and rail. The Spanish broom
turns to shadow; the gold
from the Guadarrama washes away.
Because a beautiful woman and her lover
are running away, breathless,
the full moon follows them.
The hidden train resonates
inside a huge mountain.
Barren fields, high sky.
Across granite mountains
and others of basalt,
is the sea and infinity at last.
We are going together; we are free.
Although God, as in the story
a proud king, may ride bareback
on the wind's best charger,
although he may swear to us, violently,
his vengeance,
although he may saddle thought,
free love, no one reaches it.

Today I write to you in my traveler's cell
at the hour of an imaginary rendezvous.
The heavy rain breaks the rainbow in the air,
and on the mountain its planetary sadness.
Sun and bells in the old tower.
Oh evening living and quiet
which places nothing moves next to everything moves,
childlike evening that your poet loved!
And adolescent day—
light eyes and dark muscles—
when you thought of Love, beside the fountain,
kissing your lips and holding your breasts!
Everything in this April light becomes transparent;
everything in the today of yesterday, the Yet
of which in its late hours,
time sings and tells,
is based on a single melody,
which is a chorus of evening and dawns.
For you Guiomar, this nostalgia of mine.

Canción

The moon is rising now
over the orange grove.
Venus shines like
a little crystal bird.

The sky is amber and beryl
behind the distant mountains,
and the quiet sea
like mulberry porcelain.

Now it is night in the garden—
the water in its pipes—
and it smells only of Jasmine,
the nightingale of scents.

How the war seems
to sleep from sea to sea,
while flowering Valencia
drinks the Guadalaviar!

Valencia of delicate towers
and soft nights, Valencia,
will I be with you
when I can't see you,
where sand spreads in the fields
and the violet sea grows distant?

An Afterword by James B. Hall

Any retrospective showing of artistic work in song, paint, or words on paper is an event of importance. Most especially this is true when a summary statement spans the most vital and presumably most productive years of the artist's dedication to his task; moreover, if the poetry (in this instance) has strong regional roots, and most especially roots in the Western United States, the obligation of discrimination, or description, becomes all the more important. These things being so, we read William Witherup's collection and selection of more than twenty-five years with an extraordinary respect for the implied dedication to his art.

Given the true nature of the profession of poetry (or the calling) mere dedication is never enough; otherwise, there would be more (and more interesting) poets in both England and America. Initially the social status, the Poetry Establishment's first reactions and the poet's reputed personality make a difference. In the end, however, only the words on paper seem to matter, and even the surviving body of work is charitably evaluated: Wordsworth's latter phase, for example, is not much held against him.

Even so, the circumstances of any poet's formative years are never ignored: willy-nilly, the life-patterns inform the poetry and the reader always needs all the help he or she can get. In William Witherup's "background" (as we put it) there are significant details. Seen selectively, these autobiographic items are apt guidelines—map contours—for the journey through these poems.

By accident of migration from Kansas City, Missouri, he grew up through the years of WWII and afterwards in the shadows of the Hanford, Washington, Atomic Energy installation; the livelihood of the family came from America's first plutonium processor, one of the most sinister wartime installations. Cheek-by-jowl with American technical advances lay the remnants, the shards, of another American culture—the American Indians. The implied conflict is central to both the life and the poetry. Thematically, we see the old vs. the new; the real or imagined past against the modernity of the here and now. The results of these conflicts are everywhere present: in the tragedy of lives wasted; in the irresolutions of love—or merely sex; in the pity expressed for most living things. Rhetorically the poems are often ironical by intention, a situation where one thing is said but another thing is implied; the language itself may be direct, expository, and at the same time highly metaphorical, suggestive. The voice-of-the-narrator of many of these poems (the "I" a persona close to one William Witherup) has many moods: social critic; the withdrawn man; the demonic personality; the appreciator of the small, sweet things of life; the exploiter of women; the seeker of youth gone, of time past. In conclusion, this background is an American experience, and especially of the American West of the past forty years. Witherup is a pure example of one kind of American poet and these poems are American poems in both their failures and their strengths.

To ask of a gifted poet both truth *and* resolution to all personal and national conflicts is probably unrealistic; the task is for all of American poetry, and not for the single voice of this time and of this place.

In any event, the matter of "influence" on a temperamentally unstable talent such as Witherup's is important, for does not this order of talent veer and seek direction in uncommon ways? At the risk of artificial distinction, one sees three kinds of influence in both the life and in the poems.

The divided loyalties of childhood have been mentioned: the primitive shards; the Gothic-terror of Plutonium at the ready. Attitudes toward women (shall we say mothers?) are in contrast to attitudes towards men (shall we say fathers?). Other evidence of this dichotomy is in the poetry and the restless wanderings of the poet; more could be said on this topic.

Secondly, there is the influence of literary, mentor-figures of importance; nor are these relationships always of a purely artistic nature. Early there was the unusual, by local standards, unconventional high school teacher; always, this type of teacher seems a generalist, and to have not very sound taste. They are "stimulating," innovative—within a provincial system. Later Witherup was exposed to Roethke's influence at the University of Washington: from Kahlil Gibran to Roethke and a campus visit by W. H. Auden is a long leap indeed. Later, and more purely literary, came Bly, Ginsberg and a literary style suggested by the *Sixties* (journal).

Fundamentally, Witherup's mind has a pronounced scholarly academic side; his delicately balanced sensibility seems to have yearned for Art, resolutions, contemplation, a tempered domestic life and/or the security of religious belief, and indeed he once considered the ministry as a career. What he got in the matter of influence, however, is a different matter: demonic, academic poets, and swinging Britishers on tour; village explainers and backcountry literary pretensions; the transitory, "Beat" literary models of San Francisco, persons often at odds with their own commercial motivations; imitative dramatizers of "self"; a sometimes literary program too easily understood by *Time* magazine.

Perhaps Witherup has not been entirely lucky in his literary and life-mentor influences: no one ever is, and everyone takes whatever can be used at the moment. Thus everyone gets what is deserved. In all these things, Witherup seems a pure representative of his generation. Growth, resourcefulness, and high professional standards are indeed another matter.

These things were all liberating, of course. But after liberation, what? Witherup has been in hospitals more than once for help; too often the Bridge seemed to be the only resolution to conflicts of Art and Life under modified capitalism. If these things at times nearly muted his voice, yet from these identical gifts and influences come new maturity, new strength. Very well, we now know Witherup will continue to write.

II

Although the term no longer has universal acceptance in highly disciplined literary discourse, for convenience Witherup may be called a romantic poet whose best work is in that mode—but with significant differences all his own.

The romantic touchstones are everywhere in the poems: an exploration of the primitive, both primitive lands and primitive peoples. The country-scapes are sympathetically rendered, and are sometimes threatening; the city-scapes are more often than not scenes of weakness, of evil. Thus Nature tends to be either good or benignly indifferent to man; civilization, technology, industry the opposite. The narrator of many poems seems to seek the experience of experience—and then to write about it. Through dreams come insights into reality (as in "Big Sur: December . . ."); the moon is a recurring symbol (as in "Moonwatching and Steelhead"—a fine, typical poem). These conventions Witherup often makes his own. They are also the currency of a great deal of modern and contemporary poetry, most especially in America, and too often in the sub-literary poetry of Writers' Workshops. In themselves these stalwart romantic conventions are not counter-productive; within those conventions, however, it is increasingly difficult to be original, Zen and Gary Snyder notwithstanding.

Unquestionably, William Witherup brings more to his poetry than received literary conventions even though American poetry may be still running in the shadows of Wordsworth, Byron and Shelley. His treatment, or his openness to myth, is distinct, felt, and very much a part of his concept of poetry itself. This virtue is more overt in the Indian materials; he handles, also, myths of our time.

Secondly, no poet writing today catches the complexity, the valence, the hysteria of being alone, of being up against it, of being driven by forces little understood; this feeling of isolation is Witherup Country and that well may be the most significant emotion of these past decades.

Finally, the protagonist of many of these poems combines a bottom-dog, just-getting-barely-through-this-day attitude with the compulsion to take big chances in poetry, in art: a rare, rewarding combination of personality and poetic talent.

All these traits, and everything I know of William Witherup's background, suggest he is an irregular poet: when he is good, he is very good indeed, as in the title poem, "Marian at Tassajara Springs"; when a poem fails, that event is also clear. On balance, one is drawn to the irregular poet, and most especially if one seeks larger views of country such as this, and especially the West Coast of the United States, *circa* 1984.

The drift of Witherup's poetry is encouraging. The later poems are more controlled, more tightly focused, more suggestive, more direct. The early poems are often about materials which the poet thinks *all* poetry should handle; the later poems treat matters of genuine, personal concern to a specific poet, namely, William Witherup.

And all of this accomplishment in troubled times: during Korea, Vietnam; during our new, national awareness of our debt to all Native Americans; presidential assassination, and attempts thereof; riots and looting in major cities; poetry, itself, in a revolutionary state, the crises being largely in the distribution system for all books, poetry included. No, not at all easy times for a new poet to learn, to find right answers, to mature as an artist.

Nevertheless, William Witherup has done these poems, and more. And who does not look forward to the next twenty-five years of his emergent poetry.

James B. Hall
Santa Cruz, California, 1986

William Witherup was born on March 24, 1935, in Kansas City, Missouri, the oldest of the four children of Mervyn Clyde Witherup and Nita Rose Allen. His father moved the family to eastern Washington state in 1944, where Witherup Sr. was to be employed for over thirty years as an operating engineer at the Hanford Atomic Works. James McGrath, William Witherup's high school art teacher and yearbook advisor, opened the doors of perception. Later, Witherup studied narrative writing with George Edwards at Willamette University, verse writing with Theodore Roethke at the University of Washington, verse writing with James B. Hall at the University of Oregon, and playwriting with Grant Redford at the University of Washington. Though Witherup has done some teaching, for the past five years he has made his living essentially in furniture moving and construction. Currently he is a member in good standing of Hod Carriers, Construction and General Laborers' Union, Local 291, San Rafael, California.

A LIMITED EDITION OF FIVE HUNDRED COPIES
PRINTED AND BOUND IN THE SPRING OF 1986 BY
MCNAUGHTON & GUNN, INC., ANN ARBOR, MICHIGAN.
DESIGNED AND PRODUCED BY MICHAEL SYKES AT
ARCHETYPE WEST, POINT REYES STATION, CALIFORNIA.
THE TYPE FACE IS GOUDY OLD STYLE.
ALL COPIES NUMBERED AND SIGNED
BY THE AUTHOR.

THIS IS COPY # _4/_____

William Witherup

Other Titles from Floating Island Publications

Peter Wild, *Barn Fires*
    32 pp, perfectbound, $3.00
Frank Graziano, *Desemboque*
    48 pp, perfectbound, $4.00
Christine Zawadiwsky, *Sleeping With The Enemy*
    32 pp, perfectbound, $4.00
Jeffery Beam, *The Golden Legend*
    48 pp, perfectbound, $5.00
David Hilton, *Penguins*
    24 pp, hand-sewn, $3.00
Joanne Kyger, *Up My Coast*
    24 pp, hand-sewn, $3.00
Frank Stewart, *The Open Water*
    64 pp, perfectbound, $5.00
Arthur Sze, *Dazzled*
    60 pp, perfectbound, $5.00
John Brandi, *The Cowboy from Phantom Banks*
    80 pp, smythe-sewn, $6.95
Peter Wild, *The Light on Little Mormon Lake*
    32 pp, hand-sewn, $4.00
Kirk Robertson, *Two Weeks Off*
    48 pp, hand-sewn, $5.00
Norbert Krapf, *Circus Songs*
    32 pp, hand-sewn, $4.00
Cole Swensen, *It's Alive She Says*
    88 pp, smythe-sewn, $5.00
Joan Wolf, *The Divided Sphere*
    96 pp, smythe-sewn, $5.00
Michael Conway, *The Odyssey Singer*
    88 pp, smythe-sewn, $5.00
Eugene Lesser, *Drug Abuse in Marin County*
    136 pp, smythe-sewn, $8.95
Adele Langendorf, *Denial*
    64 pp, smythe-sewn, $5.00

Floating Island I
    120 pp, smythe-sewn, $6.95
Floating Island II
    184 pp, perfectbound, $8.95
Floating Island III
    160 pp, perfectbound, $12.95